# THE
# WESTLIFE
## STORY

# THE
# WESTLIFE
## STORY

**Sarah Delmege**

BOXTREE

First published 2000 by Boxtree
an imprint of Macmillan Publishers Ltd
25 Eccleston Place London SW1W 9NF
Basingstoke and Oxford

www.macmillan.co.uk

Associated companies throughout the world

ISBN 0 7522 7145 8

9 8 7 6 5 4 3 2

A CIP catalogue record for this book is
available from the British Library.

Typeset by Blackjacks
Printed by Mackays of Chatham, PLC

# CONTENTS

# CHAPTER ONE
# WELCOME TO WESTLIFE

Ever since Westlife exploded on to the British consciousness in 1998, they've blasted the cobwebs out of the national pop scene. Nicky, Shane, Kian, Bryan and Mark have proved to be the biggest thing to hit the music business and the public in years. Their first four singles have rocketed to the top of the charts, making them the first boy band ever to have their first four singles go straight in at number one. By itself that would be amazing, but when you consider that their debut album, *Westlife*, also went straight in at number two, you can tell there's something special going on with this band. Something huge, in fact. Indeed, the only way someone might not have heard of Westlife is if they've been holed up in a cellar away from newspapers, magazines, television and the radio. It's almost impossible to open a paper or a magazine without seeing something about the fantastic five.

Even more amazingly, two years ago they were nobodies with only their dreams of one day making it big in the music industry. Now everyone knows exactly who they are. These days, Westlife are the hottest commodity on the planet. They're young, they're talented and they've worked hard to get where they are. So here's the complete story of the fabulous fivesome's rise to fame and pop stardom . . .

# CHAPTER TWO
# BRYAN

**'I'll know I'm famous when I have five Ferraris, seven houses, Cameron Diaz on my arm and a little man following me with a huge bag of money.'**

**Name**
> Bryan Nicholas McFadden

**Date of birth**
> 12 April 1980

**Place of birth**
> Dublin

**Where do you live now**
> Artane, Dublin

**Colour of eyes**
> Blue

**Height**
> 6′ 1″

**Any tattoos**
> Not yet.

**Family**
> One sister called Susan and a dog called Chip.

**Dream home**
> *Massive house in Ireland.*

**Worst class at school**
> *Irish*

**Best class at school**
> *English*

**Likes**
> *Music, females and spending money.*

**Dislikes**
> *School, reading, writing, other people's sadness – I like everybody to be happy.*

**Fave sport**
> *Soccer*

**Fave actor**
> *Leo DiCaprio*

**Fave actress**
> *Jennifer Love Hewitt*

**Fave male singer**
> *Brian Littrell*

**Fave female singer**
> *Mariah Carey*

**Best movie ever**
> Titanic

**Fave cereal**
> *Alpen*

**Fave food**
> *A fry-up from the Carlton Cafe in Sligo.*

**Fave soft drink**
> *Cola light*

**McDonald's or Burger King**
> *McDonald's*

**Fave place to chill**

> *On the beach or in a boat.*

**Fave place to visit**

> *USA*

**Fave men's perfume**

> *D&G*

**Fave women's perfume**

> *Cool Water*

**Fave football team**

> *Manchester United*

**Fave song**

> *'Something Stupid', by Frank Sinatra*

**Rule of life**

> *Live life today and deal with tomorrow when it comes.*

**U2 or B\*Witched**

> *U2*

**Backstreet Boys or Boyzone**

> *Backstreet Boys*

**Blondes or brunettes**

> *Both*

**Do you have a girlfriend**

> *No, I wish!*

**Fave one-liner**

> *Howya, love?*

**Most romantic move you've ever made**

> *I sent my ex-girlfriend's mother flowers, thanking her for bringing her daughter into the world.*

**Phrase that you use most often**

> *What's the craic!*

**'I've worked in a cash and carry store, a wine cellar and McDonald's, which was by far the worst job. I was a security guard for McDonald's in Dublin city centre and it was awful! I just stood there all day – it was so boring!'**

## Bryan's story

Bryan was born on 12 April 1980, to Mairead and Brendan McFadden. Mairead is a playschool teacher while Brendan is an area sales manager for a pharmaceutical company in Dublin. From an early age it was obvious that Bryan was destined for a life out of the ordinary. For as long as he can remember he has been singing and dancing.

Westlife's fame may still be recent but it's not the first time Bryan's hit the spotlight. When he was eight he joined the Billie Barry Stage School – Shane and Mikey from Boyzone are also former pupils, as are Edele and Keavy from B*Witched – with his sister Susan who has since become an actress, which was when he started appearing in plays and getting into dancing. Bryan loved the buzz he got from acting so much that he went twice a week for over eight years. But it was singing that really captured his heart. Like most other teenagers across the county, Bryan would spend hours posing in front of the mirror pretending to be Michael Jackson, but he never thought he'd find even a little bit of the fame that his idol had achieved. As he grew up and started buying records Bryan could only imagine what fame would be like. Although Susan was fast becoming one of Ireland's most famous young actresses, for Bryan fame was something distant, something to be hoped for but unlikely to be gained.

At school, Bryan was bright but very lazy. He hated studying and never got the exam grades he deserved. He was given a rough time by the other kids at school, and was constantly teased for being overweight. 'I had a big belly and a fat face,' he explains, which left him feeling very isolated and lonely. Every night he'd return home from school, feeling down and miserable, and pray for God to help him.

'I used to always say, "Please look down on me and bless me and tomorrow let me wake up and be normal",' he remembers.

But away from the constant taunting at Billy Barry's Stage School, Bryan could come alive and really be himself, and filled much of his free time with music. The interest in dance that he'd cultivated as a child continued and as he got older he dedicated more and more time to dancing and getting fit. He began to enjoy himself at Billy Barry's, performing, dancing and singing, and the nights out clubbing with his friends there became an endless blur of fun. And as he became more and more active, Bryan's extra weight started falling away. He was physically active every day, either at stage school learning to sing and dance, at hip hop dance classes or playing Gaelic football.

Bryan also got some part-time jobs for extra money. He drove a forklift truck one summer, and he also found work calling out the numbers in a bingo hall. The worst job he ever had was working as a security guard at the McDonald's in the centre of Dublin.

As he started to lose weight, Bryan's confidence began to soar. He followed the charts with interest, watching enviously as Boyzone's career took off. He loved acts like the Backstreet Boys, Boyz II Men and Mariah Carey. He started a few boy bands himself, but they never seemed to get much further than sitting in his house with some friends, putting on tapes and talking about what they'd do to make themselves stand out in the music scene. It wasn't a great start to a pop career, but at least Bryan was doing something and having a good time while he was at it.

Still, all good things come to an end and eventually Bryan left Billy Barry's. At the age of 17, he was doing karaoke nights and was in a band that wasn't going anywhere. But then he met two other guys, Tima and Darragh; they clicked straight away and before long they had formed their own band. They called the band Cartel, and they had great fun together, working hard and playing hard. All three boys took the band very seriously and rehearsed together every day. They played gigs all over Dublin and started to build up their own following of around 200 fans who followed them religiously from gig to gig. But they didn't have the right management and without the right people behind them there was only so far Cartel could go. Bryan wasn't sure if he'd ever achieve his dream of pop stardom.

# CHAPTER THREE
# NICKY

**'The lads say that girls want to grab hold of my bum, but I think it's probably more my blue twinkly eyes that gets them!'**

**Full name**

Nicholas Bernard James Adam Byrne

**Date of birth**

9 October 1978

**Place of birth**

Dublin

**Where do you live now**

Baldoyle, Dublin with my parents.

**Height**

5' 9½"

**Colour of eyes**

Blue

**Family**

One sister and one brother.

**Any tattoos**

None yet, but I will get one.

**Dream home**

*A big house just outside Dublin.*

**School**

*Returned to Plunket College after spending two years with Leeds United Football Club.*

**Worst class at school**

*I was never any good at maths.*

**Best class(es) at school**

*English was easy and geography wasn't bad.*

**Hobbies**

*Football and snooker.*

**Likes**

*Football, especially Man. United and Leeds 'cos I used to be the goalie in the junior team; eating out, shopping and travelling home to Ireland to see my family.*

**Dislikes**

*Smoking and nasty people.*

**Fave sports**

*Football and snooker.*

**Fave actor**

*Bruce Willis and Brad Pitt.*

**Fave actress**

*Demi Moore*

**Fave male singer**

*Phil Collins*

**Fave female singer**

*Natalie Imbruglia*

**Best movie(s) ever**

Titanic, Die Hard.

**Fave cereal**

*Sugar Puffs*

**Fave food**

*Sunday dinner*

**Fave soft drink**

*Pepsi*

**McDonald's or Burger King**

*McDonald's, definitely.*

**Fave place to chill**

*My couch in my front living room in Dublin.*

**Fave place to visit**

*The Caribbean, New York or Sydney.*

**Fave men's perfume**

*D&G*

**Fave women's perfume**

*CK Eternity*

**Fave football team**

*Manchester United*

**Fave group**

*Boyzone*

**Fave song**

*'Flying Without Wings', by Westlife!*

**Rule of Life**

*Never think that anyone's better than you and never think that you're better than anyone else.*

**U2 or B\*Witched**

*U2*

**Backstreet Boys or Boyzone**

*Boyzone*

**Blondes or brunettes**

*Depends.*

**Do you have a girlfriend**

*Yes.*

**Fave one-liner**

*How do you like your eggs in the morning?*

**Most romantic move you've ever made**

*Surprised my girlfriend by coming home unannounced after being away for two months.*

**Phrase that you use most often**

*Le Gra – it means 'with love' in Irish.*

## 'I'll know I'm famous when my mum asks me for my autograph.'

## Nicky's story

Nicky grew up in Baldoyle, in the north-east of Dublin, ten minutes away from the sea. He was part of a huge family: his mum, Yvonne, has four sisters, Betty, Marie, Con and Bernadette, who are all married with children and they often have enormous family get-togethers.

Nicky grew up going to mass every Sunday with his mother. These days his faith is still very strong, but Westlife's hectic schedule means he doesn't get to go to church very often, so he makes sure he says his prayers every night. Nicky's mum has been a huge influence on his life – she always taught him never to look down on anybody, that no one is better than him and that he wasn't any better than anyone else. It's a philosophy that's stuck with him to this day.

His dad, Nicholas, has also been a big influence in Nicky's life. He works as a painter and decorator, and is also a singer in a cabaret band called Nikki and

Studz which plays twice a week at different places around Dublin. Nicky is also very close to his sister, Gillian, 22, who works for Ryanair at Dublin airport and his brother, Adam, 10, who's in primary school.

Nicky had a very happy childhood. At the age of five, he was playing mini-league football, coached by his dad who used to be a goalie for a Dublin team. At seven he started playing in goal for Home Farm, the top schoolboy club in Ireland. Despite being incredibly talented at football he was overlooked for the Irish Schoolboy team because of his height: he was only 5′ 4″. But his manager intervened on his behalf and at the age of 15, Nicky played his first game for Ireland U15 team against Switzerland in Zurich. They won four–nil.

During this time, Nicky was also attending St Nessain's Secondary School. He worked hard at his studies, but always found time to have a laugh in class and his angelic looks meant he usually got away with it. Despite being so busy with football, Nicky was also developing a passion for music. He loved singing, but was far too shy to perform in front of other people. His sister Gillian loved pop music, and through her Nicky started listening to bands like A-Ha, Bros and Take That. When he was fourteen, he watched as a new Irish band called Boyzone made their debut on *The Late Late Show*. He videoed the show for Gillian, and the two of them watched the tape over and over again.

Around this time the big professional clubs started showing an interest in Nicky. He had offers to sign for

Newcastle and Everton, but it was Leeds that offered him the best deal, even flying his parents to England to see where their son would be working and living if he signed to the club. After much discussion, Nicky decided he'd leave school and go to Leeds. He hadn't yet taken his exams but his parents agreed that he should go. If things didn't work out he could always take his leaving exam later.

Nicky was extremely nervous about moving to Leeds. He knew what a great opportunity it would be, but he hated leaving his family and friends behind. The night before his flight Nicky sat in bed crying his heart out, while his dad sat beside him trying to calm him down.

But once he was in Leeds, Nicky knew he had made the right decision. He lived in a huge house with nine of the other players and had a great time. Unfortunately, things didn't work out as he'd hoped. Although he was picked for the first team squad during his first season at Leeds, Nicky's confidence took a knocking through one of the football coaches. 'He was a hard man and the whole experience was awful. It wasn't just me it affected, other players suffered as well,' he remembers.

By the second year, the problems really started for Nicky. The youth team were moved into the new institution set up by former manager Howard Wilkinson at the back of Leeds' training ground – a self-contained centre where the apprentices would eat, drink, sleep, go to school, play football and socialize. Nicky didn't enjoy the experience at all. 'We were the first group to live at the training ground in Thorp Arch,' says Nicky. 'It's right across from Wealstun Prison and the lads used to call it "the other prison"'.

Then, towards the end of his contract, Nicky was told that Leeds wouldn't be keeping him on because he was still too small. Nicky was devastated: he'd slogged his heart out for two years, all for nothing. His former team-mates still insist he could have achieved just as much fame as a footballer. 'He could have gone all the way,' says Jonathan Woodgate, 'his shot-stopping is second to none. I think he could have got a Premiership job. He has got the attitude to do it as well.'

Nicky went for trials at Cambridge and Scarborough, but his heart was no longer in football and he decided to go back to Dublin. 'The goalkeeping coach, John Burridge, told me not to give it up,' says Nicky now. 'David Seaman was released by Leeds and there are so many people who didn't make it at first but didn't give up hope. I wanted to, but I didn't want to go through what I went through at Leeds again.'

Instead Nicky got a job in a clothes shop called Alias Tom, and played football for the League of Ireland, although it was hard knowing that some of his friends in Leeds were now professional football players.

'It was a difficult time for me,' he says now. 'I cried. I cried a lot. I went home and I hit a brick wall. After three or four months I was ringing my old friends and they had all bought new cars and they were all in the first team squad. It was really, really tough.'

Nicky started to feel like a failure, but his mum and dad were there, supporting him and encouraging him whenever he felt down. Determined to move on, he set to work and passed his leaving certificate at Plunket College in Dublin. While he was studying, Nicky bought a karaoke machine and started doing a series of karaoke nights in bars and local parties. The response to his appearances was amazing and he longed to be in a proper band, though he didn't have a clue how to go about it. So instead, he put his dreams of pop stardom behind him and decided he would join the Gardai and become a policeman. Fortunately for the future of pop music, round about that time one of Nicky's aunts heard about an audition for a boy band – the event which would change Nicky's life beyond his wildest dreams.

# CHAPTER FOUR
# SHANE

'Seriously, it's very hard to have girlfriends as we're away so much – that's the reality of it and it's going to get worse before it gets better.'

**Full name**
*Shane Steven Filan*
**Date of birth**
*5 July 1979*
**Place of birth**
*Sligo, Ireland*
**Where do you live now**
*Sligo and on the road with the band.*
**Eyes**
*Hazel/green*
**Height**
*5' 9"*
**Family**
*Three brothers and three sisters.*
**Any tattoos**
*No.*

## ▶ THE WESTLIFE STORY

**Dream home**
*A very big place with a swimming pool.*

**School**
*Summerhill College*

**Worst class at school**
*Science*

**Best class(es) at school**
*English and maths.*

**Hobbies**
*Horse-riding, snooker, pitch and putt.*

**Likes**
*Shopping, girls, going out with friends, horses and singing.*

**Dislikes**
*Insects, snakes, rude people.*

**Fave sport**
*Football and horse-riding.*

**Fave actor**
*Tom Cruise*

**Fave actress**
*Catherine Zeta Jones*

**Fave male singer**
*George Michael*

**Fave female singer**
*Mariah Carey*

**Best movie ever**
Titanic

**Fave cereal**
*Cornflakes*

**Fave food**
*Spaghetti*

**Fave soft drink**
> *Coca cola*

**McDonald's or Burger King**
> *Both.*

**Fave place to chill**
> *At home.*

**Fave place to visit**
> *Tenerife*

**Fave men's perfume**
> *Polo Sport/Ralph Lauren*

**Fave women's perfume**
> *Beautiful/Chloe*

**Fave football team**
> *Liverpool*

**Fave song**
> *'I Believe I Can Fly', by R Kelly.*

**Rule of Life**
> *You only live once, so live a good life.*

**U2 or B*Witched**
> *U2*

**Backstreet Boys or Boyzone**
> *Both.*

**Blondes or brunettes**
> *Both.*

**Fave one-liner**
> *Too many to mention!*

**Most romantic move ever**
> *Buy a lot of balloons for your girlfriend's bedroom.*

**Phrase you use most often**
> *You know what I mean.*

**'I felt weird. I was dead paranoid about it. I thought, is everyone staring at me, is it obvious?' Shane on having to wear make-up.**

## Shane's story

Shane was born in Sligo, the youngest of seven children. His oldest brother is Finbar, 30, an industrial engineer. Then there's Peter, 29, a paediatric doctor in Dublin. Next there's Yvonne, 28, a teacher at Mercy College girls' school in Sligo. After her is Liam, 27, who helps run the family horse business. Then there's Denise, 23, a physiotherapist at a Dublin hospital. After Denise comes Mairead, 21, a marketing manager in Dublin. Shane is the baby of the family.

Shane's dad, Peter, has always owned restaurants, and together with Shane's mum, Mae, and his uncle, Luke, opened a small restaurant called The Mayfair. Shortly afterwards they opened the Carlton Cafe in Castle Street. For as long as Shane could remember, the family lived in the house above the restaurant.

These days, Shane's mum looks after the restaurant while his dad runs a horse business which he runs with Liam. They buy horses, look after them and then sell them.

As the baby of the family, Shane was always spoilt more than the others. Although he was short for his age, he never got picked on by other lads because his big brothers were always on hand to sort any trouble out.

From an early age, Shane loved to sing. The first record he ever owned was 'Uptown Girl' by Billy Joel, which his mum had bought for him on tape. Before long he knew all the words and would spend hours singing along to them.

But it was Michael Jackson who really changed Shane's life. Shane started to dress like him and learnt all Michael's dance moves, spending hours alone in his room teaching himself to moonwalk. When he was twelve, Shane went along for auditions for the musical *Grease* at the Hawkswell Theatre in Sligo. There wasn't really a role for a boy his age, but the producer was so impressed by Shane's audition that he created a special part for him to sing 'We Go Together'. It was then that Shane fell in love with performing.

When he went to secondary school at Summerhill College, Shane really got into acting and singing. The teachers soon recognized his talent and Shane was given most of the lead roles. It was through the musicals that Shane got to know Mark and Kian.

Shane was determined to start a band. He and his friend, Michael, wanted to start a four-piece band called S4, but had trouble getting anyone interested. Even Kian, who was into heavy rock music at the time, laughed at the idea when Shane asked him to join! Michael and Shane got another two boys interested in the band instead; they fixed a time for the rehearsal, but the two other lads never showed up. Shane thought that was the end for his hopes of a pop career.

# CHAPTER FIVE
# KIAN

'A few months ago, I was always asking Louis, our manager, "When are we going to do this, when are we going to do that?" and he said, "Look Kian, in a year's time you'll be asking me, 'When are we going to have some time off?'"'

**Full name**

Kian John Francis Egan

**Date of birth**

29 April 1980

**Place of birth**

Sligo, Ireland

**Where do you live now**

On the road.

**Eyes**

Blue

**Family**

Three brothers and three sisters.

**Any tattoos**

The Chinese symbol for spirit and soul.

**Dream home**

*A big house in Hollywood.*

**School**

*Summerhill College*

**Worst class at school**

*Maths*

**Best class at school**

*Art*

**Hobbies**

*Snooker, pitch and putt.*

**Likes**

*Performing on stage, a good night out and being in Westlife.*

**Dislikes**

*Sushi and rude people.*

**Fave sport**

*Basketball*

**Fave actor**

*Brad Pitt*

**Fave actress**

*Cameron Diaz*

**Fave male singer**

*Brian Littrell*

**Fave female singer**

*Celine Dion*

**Best movie ever**

Titanic

**Fave cereal**

*Frosties*

**Fave food**

*Steak and chips*

**Fave soft drink**
> *Seven Up*

**McDonald's or Burger King**
> *McDonald's*

**Fave place to chill**
> *In front of TV.*

**Fave men's perfume**
> *Joop*

**Fave women's perfume**
> *Loads of them.*

**Fave football team**
> *Leeds United*

**Fave music**
> *Backstreet Boys, Boyzone, Five.*

**Fave song**
> *'Baby, One More Time', by Britney Spears.*

**Rule of life**
> *Treat everybody the same way you want to be treated.*

**U2 or B*Witched**
> *U2*

**Backstreet Boys or Boyzone**
> *Backstreet Boys*

**Blondes or brunettes**
> *Both.*

**Fave one-liner**
> *I don't use any.*

**Most romantic move ever**
> *Too many to give away.*

**Phrase you use most often**
> *Alone.*

**'The days are gone when you'd just put five good-looking lads on stage and that'd be it. You need to be talented and that's why we'll make it.'**

**'I'm the cheeky one of the group. I'm not complaining if people want to call me sexy.'**

## Kian's story

Kian also grew up as part of a huge family. His dad, Kevin, is an electrician for the ESB – the Irish Electricity Board – while his mum, Patricia, is a full-time mum and housewife. Kian has six brothers and sisters. First there is Viv, 30, who works as town planner in Roscommon; then there is Gavin, 28, a secondary school teacher and music lecturer at Sheffield University. Fenella is 24, she's a legal secretary with two children. After Fenella comes Tom, 22, who is studying architecture at college and is the bassist in a rock band called Fiction. After Tom comes Marielle, who's 13 and at school. Then, last but not least, is the baby of the family, Colm, who's only four.

Kian shared a room with Tom when they were growing up. Like any other brothers the two of them would fight like anything, but they were also extremely close and would often hang out together.

At the age of four, Kian entered his first talent competition, in which he recited a poem called 'Whispers'. He won, and was presented with a little trophy that he still has today.

Kian's whole family are very musical and he grew up surrounded by music. His sisters played the violin and Kian learnt the piano from Gavin who was a part-time piano teacher. But it was rock music that really captured Kian's heart. He'd spend hours in his room, listening to tunes on the radio and teaching himself to play them on the guitar. Every evening the Egan household would rock to the various sound of the family practising on their different instruments.

Kian dreamed of becoming a rock star. He loved bands like Metallica, Guns N' Roses, Iron Maiden and Bon Jovi. He formed a band with four friends – they wrote a few songs, but mostly performed cover versions of rock songs. They grew their hair long and dreamed of becoming the next Metallica.

Kian also started doing musicals at the Hawkswell Theatre and he discovered a love of performing. During a performance of *Grease*, Kian got to know Shane; the two immediately clicked, but they didn't think much of each other's musical tastes. Shane really wasn't into rock and Kian couldn't understand why Shane would want to be in a boy band of all things.

But Kian's life changed when he heard the kind of music boy band Take That were producing. He began to listen to more pop music, watched Boyzone's career with avid interest and fell in love with the songs the Backstreet Boys produced. The way they looked, the way they sang, their clothes, everything. For the first time, Kian was left with no doubt about what he wanted to do with his life.

# CHAPTER SIX
# MARK

**'I'll know I'm famous when someone I think is famous asks for my autograph.'**

**Full Name**
> Mark Michael Patrick Feehily

**Date of birth**
> 28 May 1980

**Place of birth**
> Sligo, Ireland

**Where do you live now**
> Sligo, Ireland

**Height**
> 5' 11"

**Colour of eyes**
> Blue

**Family**
> Two brothers.

**Any tattoos**
> Nope.

**Dream house**
> Big house with swimming pool and tennis court in Sligo.

**School**

*Summerhill College*

**Worst class(es) at school**

*Irish and woodwork.*

**Best class(es) at school**

*French and home economics.*

**Hobbies**

*Tennis, football, snooker, chilling out.*

**Likes**

*Chillin' with my mates, singing and partying.*

**Dislikes**

*Being tied down, having too much on my plate, narrow-minded people, smoking.*

**Fave sport(s)**

*Football and tennis.*

**Fave actor**

*Eddie Murphy*

**Fave actress**

*Lisa Kudrow (Phoebe in* Friends*)*

**Fave male singer**

*Michael Jackson*

**Fave female singer**

*Mariah Carey*

**Best movie(s) ever**

The Nutty Professor, Titanic.

**Fave cereal**

*Rice Krispies or Weetabix.*

**Fave food**

*Steak and chips.*

**Fave soft drink**

*Fanta Lemon*

**McDonald's or Burger King**

    *McDonald's*

**Fave place to chill**

    *On the couch in front of TV.*

**Fave place to visit**

    *Home (Sligo)*

**Fave men's perfume**

    *Hugo Boss*

**Fave women's perfume**

    *Calvin Klein*

**Fave football team**

    *Liverpool*

**Fave music**

    *Everything*

**Fave songs**

    *'Man in the Mirror', by Michael Jackson and*
    *'Without You', by Mariah Carey.*

**Rule of life**

    *Money isn't everything, but happiness is.*

**U2 or B\*Witched**

    *U2*

**Backstreet Boys or Boyzone**

    *Boyzone*

**Blondes or brunettes**

    *Brunettes*

**Do you have a girlfriend**

    *No, too young – I have many.*

**Fave one-liner**

    *Here love, here's two kroner – ring your mum and tell*
    *her you won't be home!*

**Most romantic move you've ever made**

*Flowers, disco, dinner, home to bed!*

**Phrase that you use most often**

Well buddy, what's the craic? (Irish for fun)

**'It's very scary when we see all these people working so hard for us and we do think, what if we let them down.'**

## Mark's story

Mark's mum, Marie, is a civil servant and works in the Department of Agriculture. His dad, Oliver, was brought up on a farm in an area just outside Sligo, which is where Mark was brought up and still lives, surrounded by beautiful fields and countryside that spreads as far as the eye can see. These days his dad owns a window company. Mark's the eldest boy in his family. After him comes Barry, 14, who's still at school. Then there's Colin, who is nine and also at school.

Mark went to St Patrick's National School, but he wasn't a star pupil – in fact he'd spend most of his time staring out of the classroom window, day-dreaming. He loved tennis and practised every single day. He dreamt of becoming a professional player, but there just weren't the facilities or the coaches available in Sligo to help him reach the necessary standard of playing. So Mark decided to give up his dreams of playing professionally and started playing just for fun.

He also started at a new school, Summerhill College. His previous school had only had about 300 children; suddenly Mark found himself at a huge school with over 1,000 schoolmates. Scared that the other pupils would laugh at him for being a farmer's son, Mark didn't make much effort to find new friends, preferring instead to stick to those he knew from his last school. Shy and reserved, it took him a long while to settle down at Summerhill.

Outside of school, though, Mark could relax and become himself. Every Sunday evening he and his family would go to his grandparents' house where everyone would take it in turns to get up and do a party piece. Mark loved these cosy family evenings and waited impatiently for his turn as it gave him a chance to stand up and sing. He may have been shy at school, in front of people he didn't know very well, but when he opened his mouth to sing, he forgot about everything else and just became caught up in the moment. His parents noticed their eldest son's natural talent and encouraged him to enter talent competitions. He once won £50 in a competition – a lot of money to an eight-year-old.

One of Mark's favourite pastimes was going to watch musicals at the local theatres. He'd settle down in his seat and lose himself in the magic of it all, wishing that it was him under the spotlight.

Mark went along to some auditions at the Hawkswell Theatre and soon was appearing in shows like *Scrooged* and *West Side Story*. It was the most exciting thing that had ever happened to him. He also got involved in the school productions at Summerhill College. When they decided to put on *Grease*, Mark met Shane and Kian. Mark sang three solos and he'd never felt such a buzz. From that moment on, he knew he wanted to become a singer.

Mark had a part-time job in a sports show to earn some extra money, but the job meant he couldn't spare the time to get involved with musicals. After much soul-searching he decided to leave his job and make singing his priority. It would prove to be one of the best decisions he ever made.

# CHAPTER SEVEN
# WESTLIFE ON
## EACH OTHER

## THE OTHERS ON NICKY

### What's the best thing about Nicky?

**Shane** He's very strong-minded and says exactly what he wants without pussy-footing around.

**Kian** He's very generous and although he looks out for himself, he makes sure he watches out for everybody else around him as well.

**Bryan** He'd do anything for anyone and he's the most mature out of all of us.

### What's his worst habit?

**Shane** He thinks he's always right! You could tell him that black is black and he'd argue that it's white!

**Bryan** He's got a fiery temper on him.

### What does he worry about?

**Mark** Everything from what we're doing tomorrow to whether the band will be successful or not.

## Is he free with his money or is he a bit of a meanie?

**Shane** He's not too bad, but he does like spending his cash on designer clothes. Actually, we're as bad as each other!

**Bryan** He spends his money, but he watches where it's going at the same time.

## THE OTHERS ON KIAN

## What's the best thing about Kian?

**Nicky** He's a really give-and-take guy, he'll sit and talk to you about anything. He's always got time for people.

**Bryan** He's the big smoocher of the band and he'll always have a chat with the ladies. I don't think he'll ever get married because he wouldn't be able to stick with just one girl.

## What's his worst habit?

**Nicky** He's the one that our manager, Louis, or our record company get in contact with when they need to speak to the band. So his phone is always red hot and he'll snap at you because he feels the pressure a bit too much sometimes.

**Bryan** Yeah, he can be too quick to jump down your throat, but if I always had management hassling me then I'd probably jump down everybody's throat too.

### What does he worry about?

**Nicky** He probably worries about what the management are going to say if we've done something wrong, because it's him that gets hassled.

### What makes him blush?

**Nicky** Probably when you mention Britney Spears: he can't wait to meet her.

### Is he free with his money or a bit of a meanie?

**Mark** He minds his money – he makes sure he's got enough to get by, but he's generous as well.

**Nicky** He's financially careful, but he does end up spending all his money on phone bills.

## THE OTHERS ON MARK

### What's the best thing about Mark?

**Nicky** He's really quiet and doesn't open up to you unless he really knows you. Mark's a very private person, but when he gets into one of his mischievous moods then there's no stopping him.

**Shane** He's got a great personality. Although he's all quiet when you're having a conversation, he'll listen until the end and then he'll just chip in something hilarious.

### What's his worst habit?

**Bryan** He farts on photoshoots! Oh, and he's useless at getting out of bed in the morning – in fact I've never met anyone who's so bad. We'll be leaving at 8am and he'll still be in bed at 7.55am. He's a nightmare.

### What does he worry about?

**Nicky** Probably about getting up in the morning – one day he'll miss a flight because he doesn't get up on time.

**Shane** He's probably the same as me – worrying about when he's going to see his family next.

## THE OTHERS ON BRYAN

### What's the best thing about Bryan?

**Kian** He's a bit of a softie and he gets very slushy when it comes to girls, but he's a lovely bloke.

**Nicky** Bryan's really, really funny, but he can be serious. If I have a problem I'll always chat to him. He's a nice guy.

### What's his worst habit?

**Nicky** He does live life on the edge a bit too much sometimes.

**Kian** Sometimes he slags people off too much.

### What does he worry about?

**Shane** Probably about spending all his money – he doesn't think about how much he's got until it's too late.

**Nicky** He worries about how the band's going to go – is it going to flop? Will it be successful?

### What makes him blush?

**Mark** He blushes when he talks to a girl that he fancies. He'll go just like a beetroot!

## THE OTHERS ON SHANE

### What's the best thing about Shane?

**Kian** He's the most easy-going one in the band. He's sensible, but enjoys a good laugh as well.

**Nicky** He's the most perfect singer I've ever heard. He learns from our manager, Ronan Keating, and you can't have a better teacher than that.

**Bryan** He's very encouraging and before we go on stage he makes sure we all know what we're doing. He's very motivating.

### What's his worst habit?

**Nicky** He doesn't pay attention all the time – it's not that he's ignoring you, but it's like he's in another world.

### What does he worry about?

**Bryan** I don't think that Shane worries about anything, he's so positive about everything and that's great for the rest of us.

### What makes him blush?

**Mark** If he ever hits a wrong note, which is very rare.

### Is he free with his money or is he a bit of a meanie?

**Nicky** He does spend it, but he's not too free with it; he's sensible.

# CHAPTER EIGHT
# THE BEGINNING

During the summer of 1996, 17-year-old Shane was picked for the lead part of Danny in the musical *Grease* at Summerhill College. Kian was chosen to play Kenickie and Mark was to play Vince Fontaine. Shane's friend Michael Garrett, Derek Lacey and an older boy, Graham Keighon, were also picked to play the parts of the leather-wearing T-birds, Danny's gang.

Practically the whole of Sligo saw the show, which was a massive success, and as a result the boys soon developed a huge base of fans. *Grease* provided the ideal platform for them to test their latest moves on a responsive and often adoring audience. The six boys loved the buzz they got from performing on stage and it wasn't long before they decided to form a band of their own.

They spent hours at each other's houses, working on cover versions and putting together some dance moves. When they'd built up a thirty-minute set they decided they were ready for their first gig. This was to take place at the Southern Hotel, after a fashion show. The boys, who had decided on the name Six As One, were a huge hit with the crowd. From the moment they walked on stage, dressed casually in different coloured tops, the crowd went mad. Girls screamed and shouted for more. The six boys loved the attention and by the time they finished their set, the one thing they were all sure of was that this was something they wanted to do more of.

They were determined to make their band work and spent hours working on their songs and practising choreography. They added new songs and dance moves and Mark and Shane wrote a song called 'Together Girl Forever' and performed at several more small venues around Sligo. During this time the boys decided that they weren't happy with the name and decided to change it. After much discussion they decided on IOU: it sounded different, modern and catchy.

The band generated an incredible amount of interest locally. Sligo had never seen anything like them before. Six boys who could sing in key and in harmony, who could fill a stage with personality and entertain just by being themselves. They were sexy, smart and they had style. Girls fell in love with the six boys wherever they went.

During this time, two local men were closely involved behind the scenes with IOU as unofficial managers. They were more than happy with all the attention that was being paid to the new boy band. They had the band's future all mapped out, everything formulated, weighed and sorted out. They wanted the six boys to sign a contract, so that they would get a slice of the profits if they boys took off. However the boys weren't sure if they should stick with their management and go along with all their plans; Shane in particular wasn't happy about signing. It was a situation with no easy solution. There was no doubt that the boys were grateful for all the help the two Sligo men had given them, but the fact was, they'd outgrown everything the men had had in mind for them. They'd moved past all that and signing such a contract could ruin all their chances for fame. The boys were smart enough to know that they needed a manager with experience and connections if they really were going to make it. But they also knew the chances of finding such a manager were slim. After all, although the boys had a huge following in Sligo, and had even released 'Together Girl Forever' on a small independent record company, outside their home town they were nobody.

However, Shane's mum, Mae, had seen the band's potential and was determined that the boys should find a new manager. She quickly cast around for a person who might be interested. It didn't take her long to come up with a suitable candidate – Louis Walsh.

Louis Walsh had been around the music business for quite a while. He had taken five lads from Dublin and turned them into Boyzone, one of the biggest boy bands of all time. As far as Ireland was concerned Louis Walsh was the best manager around, and Mae Filan was determined that he should manage her son's band. It wasn't an easy task, but Mae had made up her mind. She wrote letters, sent the IOU CD and left message after message on Louis's answer machine. There was no response, but Mae wasn't about to give up. Every day she'd pick up the phone and call his office; one morning in February her perseverance paid off when she finally got through to Louis himself. She told him about the band and, although Mae's call was just one of hundreds of calls Louis received every day, she somehow convinced him to see the band. IOU's lives were about to change forever.

Mae could hardly contain her excitement. She immediately rang Shane, who was staying with his sister, and told him to ring Louis immediately. 'I thought she was winding me up – so did the rest of the band when I told them,' he laughs.

A meeting was set in a local nightclub called POD. The six lads spent ages choosing what they were to wear: they knew they needed to look the part, to convince Louis that they really could be pop stars. However, when they got to the club, the bouncer wouldn't let them in at first! Fortunately for the future of pop, Louis was waiting by the entrance and waved the nervous boys through. It wasn't all good news though: Louis told them he was far too busy with Boyzone to manage them. But he said he'd help them find a manager and that they could support Boyzone on tour. The boys left the club floating on air. 'We ran down the street screaming our heads off,' remembers Kian. 'It was such a buzz.'

With Louis on board, the boys had no doubt that things would start to take off. They were right. A week later Louis rang them and told them he'd got them the support slot on a Backstreet Boys concert.

The American ambassadors of pop were playing two gigs at one of Dublin's biggest venues, the RDS Arena. The IOU boys were such huge fans of the Backstreet Boys that they already had tickets to one of the shows. They couldn't believe that not only would they be seeing their heroes play, they'd also be performing on the same stage as them! Shane and Kian stared at each other in disbelief, before starting to jump up and down, hugging each other. In just a week, their lives had changed beyond their wildest dreams.

There was little time for celebrations however, as the concert was only a week away. It was time to get down to some serious rehearsals. Louis had told the boys to prepare three songs, so they sat down and began a weeding-out process of their set. They wanted the very best, the strongest material for their appearance. After much deliberation, they decided on 'Together Girl Forever', 'Everlasting Love' and a cover of the Who's 'Pinball Wizard'. The music was professionally recorded on to a DAT.

Every evening the boys would gather round at one of their houses and run through their songs and dance routines. Each little mistake had to be criticized and corrected. It was a tedious business, but the boys knew just what a big chance they'd been given and they weren't about to blow it. Then it was time to sort out clothes. They knew that how they looked counted just as much as the way they sang, and they were determined that although they might not have the money to buy designer clothes, they were still going to look as sharp and stylish as Boyzone do in their Gucci and Dolce and Gabbana suits. In the end they decided on matching cream coloured trousers with each member wearing a different coloured top.

The local media were quick to jump on the story. The *Evening Herald* ran stories on the band and local radio stations mentioned the gig over and over again. When the day of the concert finally arrived – Tuesday 17 March – the boys could hardly contain their excitement.

'We were about to go from performing in front of one hundred people to playing to a crowd of seven thousand. It was amazing,' remembers Shane. As they arrived at the venue they couldn't believe the number of fans who were already milling about. And as they made their way backstage, the Backstreet Boys came over for a chat and to wish them the best of luck with the concert and their careers.

IOU's two shows went brilliantly. The girls in the audience couldn't get enough of them and the boys had never felt such a buzz playing to such a huge crowd. They didn't think things could get any better.

'We saw the reaction the Backstreet Boys got, the fame, the success, the fans,' says Mark. 'We wanted all that for ourselves.'

But there was still another surprise to come. Louis had studied the band closely from backstage. As he watched their routine, he noticed the extremely positive reaction from the crowd. Girls in the audience were going mad for them. Although they needed a lot of work, he saw a convincing pop act with plenty of talent and a huge hunger for success. By the end of the second concert Louis had become convinced of the boys' future as pop stars, and it was then he decided the time was right to manage them. The boys couldn't believe it, but before Louis's announcement had time to sink in, he broke the bad news: he would only manage the band as a five-piece – one of them would have to go.

The boys were devastated. How on earth could they make such a horrible decision? But deep down in their hearts they knew Louis was right. The five-piece pop band is a hugely successful template that's been used over and over again in the pop business by bands such as the Spice Girls, Take That, Boyzone and the Backstreet Boys. After much soul-searching it was decided that Derek would be the one to leave. Shane had to break the news. It was one of the hardest things he ever had to do, especially as Derek was one of his closest friends. Tough as it was, the boys knew they had no choice if they were to stick with their dream of becoming pop stars. If they didn't lose a member, Louis wouldn't manage them, and if Louis didn't take over at the reins, they knew they had little or no chance of making it. They also knew that the same thing had happened to many groups before them. Boyzone had originally had a different line-up, as had the Spice Girls and the Backstreet Boys. It had even happened to the Beatles, the most famous band of all time.

The remaining five boys didn't feel good about the decision they had made. However, they were more determined than ever to make it and to show that the decision, tough as it was, had been the right one.

# CHAPTER NINE
# THE NEXT STEP

Next on the agenda was meeting record companies to try and secure a deal. Under Louis's watchful eye, Shane, Kian, Michael and Graham recorded two more original songs, 'Good Thing' and 'Everybody Knows', on a demo tape so that he could play it to his contacts in the music industry. The boys also practised and repractised their set, so that they were absolutely note perfect.

If that wasn't excitement enough, Boyzone front-man Ronan Keating was becoming more and more involved with the band. Boyzone had always been role models for the boys and they couldn't believe that Ronan was happy to help choose their songs and give them advice. For his part, Ronan saw the band's potential – in fact he was reminded of himself and the other Boyzone lads during their early days. Louis watched as an incredibly strong bond began to grown between Ronan and the other boys, and he offered Ronan the chance to become co-manager of the band – an offer Ronan was only too happy to accept.

'Being co-manager may sound pretty serious, but I'm not at all like a boss to them,' Ronan explains. 'I'm their friend and adviser and I help with the artistic side of the group. From the very beginning I could see they were a truly talented bunch of guys and I was thrilled to be part of the team.'

Ronan sat down with the boys and told them exactly what they could expect from life as would-be pop stars. 'The boys certainly deserve to be huge. They are genuinely talented, have great voices and have a really professional approach to their work. The one thing I stressed to them is that there is a lot of hard work involved in being a pop performer. You can not imagine how much work is involved. Boyzone didn't know what lay ahead when we started out. Nobody prepared us for the late nights, early mornings, travelling and never seeing your family and friends. Maybe we were better off not knowing.'

But from working with the boys, Ronan could see they had exactly the right attitude. They were willing to give up their lives for a few years and be totally dedicated to making the group a success around the world. And that's what it takes: dedication, hard work, team spirit and, most of all, a positive attitude. And of course the boys were only too happy to have Ronan on board. 'Ronan's been really cool,' says Kian.

It's also important to get on well with people. As Ronan still reminds the boys, 'Be nice to people on the way up because you're going to meet them on the way down.' But all of the boys were a friendly bunch anyway so that certainly wouldn't be a problem for them.

IOU now had a team behind them that could give them the chance of the success they really deserved and they were feeling more and more positive about the way things were starting to happen for them. A meeting had been scheduled with Simon Cowell, one of the most respected A&R men in the industry. Simon had handled the careers of a number of artists, including the boy band Five, and IOU hoped he would be prepared to do the same for them.

The boys turned up at the Dublin hotel with Louis a mixture of nerves and excitement. After all, this could be the day when they would secure a record deal and their lives would change beyond all recognition. Unfortunately things didn't go to plan. Simon listened to the boys sing, then disappeared for a chat with Louis. When Louis reappeared, they could see from his face that the news wasn't good. Louis sat down and broke the news to them. Simon wasn't interested in signing the band, although he thought he might be able to use Kian and Mark in another group at some point.

The boys were gutted. They had been so sure that this would be it, that Simon would take one look at IOU and would be begging to sign them on the dotted line.

But they were determined not to let this first knock-back stop them. They were prepared to do whatever it took to make sure the band made it to the top. Unfortunately, this meant making more tough decisions. The band obviously wasn't working as a unit: all the ingredients for pop success weren't yet in place and until the perfect recipe was found all the boys' places in the band were in danger. It was decided that Graham would have to go: the age gap between him and the rest of the boys was just too big (he was almost twenty-two at the time) and it jarred on stage. Of course, it was devastating for Graham to have come so far for nothing, but he knew the band as a whole had to come before any individual members and so after just two more Sligo gigs he left the band.

# CHAPTER TEN
# FINDING A REPLACEMENT

Now the band had to find someone to step into Graham's shoes. Not just anyone would do: they needed someone with the right chemistry to blend in with the rest of them. It was decided that they'd hold open auditions at the Red Box in Dublin. Adverts were placed in Dublin newspapers and local radio stations gave out information. On the day of the auditions over 300 wannabe pop stars lined up, ready to strut their stuff. Just listening to them all, hearing them talk and letting them run through their numbers took hours. Many were awful. Of those who were good, plenty just didn't have the kind of personality or looks that IOU needed. Exactly what they wanted was still cloudy, but the boys felt they'd know it when they saw it.

A number of guys were called back and given the chance to perform at greater length. Louis, Ronan and the IOU lads watched closely. How did they project themselves? Did they have that mysterious and elusive star quality? After all, songs could be bought, routines could be choreographed, but a guy either had charisma, something that set him apart and focused eyes on him, or he didn't. It's not something you can fake, force or buy.

Among the shortlisted hopefuls were Nicky and Bryan. Nicky's auntie had told him about the audition and he rang up one of his local radio stations to find out the details. He recorded three songs in his living room on his karaoke machine – 'Isn't It A Wonder', 'She Moves Through The Fair' and 'The Town I Know So Well' – then sent off his tape with a photograph. A few days later he received a phone call inviting him to the audition.

Bryan, meanwhile, was still in the band Cartel. He wanted Louis Walsh to become the band's manager and had managed to reach him on the telephone. Louis wasn't interested but, impressed by Bryan's perseverance, invited him to the auditions for IOU. Bryan spent hours agonizing over whether or not he should go to the audition. Although he felt he was letting Cartel down, he knew it was too good an opportunity to miss.

He was right. At the second Red Box audition, the shortlist was quickly whittled down to six and then just to two: Nicky and Bryan. As the two boys sung their hearts out, no one watching could decide between them. They were asked to sing with the whole group to try and work out which one added the most. The two boys had very different voices, but both brought something different and something special to the band as a whole. It seemed an impossible choice.

Louis decided that both Nicky and Bryan would spend a few days with the band in Sligo, to see how they got on with the rest of the lads. If one of them fitted in better than the other, the choice would be clear. But Nicky and Bryan both got on brilliantly with everyone and each other. They quickly fitted in, laughing and mucking around with the others. But it was more than that: Bryan and Nicky might have known how to have a good laugh, but they were both professionals at heart and were obviously hungry for success. The obvious decision was to invite both of them to join the band, but it had already been decided that the band wouldn't work as a six-piece. Another tough decision had to be made. All six boys were summoned back to the Red Box where Michael was told he would have to leave the band. Of course, he was devastated, as were the other band members. Not only had Michael been in the band since the beginning, he had grown up with Kian, Shane and Mark. But difficult as it was, they knew they had to go with the best line-up. The band was the most important thing and the boys couldn't let personal feelings get in the way of professional decisions.

Louis knew that in much the same way as IOU had been remoulded to become a group, he would also have to build a team of people to give the boys the chance to be as successful as the deserved to be. He approached his old friend Anto Byrne to become IOU's tour manager. The pair had known each other for nearly twenty years, and Anto had worked with such big acts as Irish superstar, Van Morrison, Annie Lennox and Julian Lennon. Anto came to meet the boys and they immediately clicked. Like Ronan and Louis before him, he saw the potential in the boys and recognized their passion and determination. More importantly, he liked them as people: in fact, the friendship between the band and Anto has become so strong that he's often referred to as the sixth member. Anto was there to travel with them and make sure that from the moment the boys got up in the morning until they were tucked up safely in bed, all the little niggles that are part of a pop star's daily life were ironed out as quickly and easily as possible.

Now the core team was in place and work could begin on building IOU into pop superstars. But although these people were necessary in putting the band together and setting them on the right road, acting as contacts, friends and mentors, it's important to remember that the five lads would never have made it if they didn't have the necessary talent.

With all the parts put together perfectly, they had so much going for them that it was impossible to believe they wouldn't go straight to the top. But there was still a distance to go and plenty of work to be done. It was time for the new band to make their first official outing. In July the boys headlined at the annual Beat On The Streets roadshow around Ireland. The boys had already built up a hard-core base of female fans who followed IOU from roadshow to roadshow. The boys loved performing on stage in front of their fans and the reaction they got was amazing. Everywhere they went girls shouted out their names and tried to get close to them. But it was an odd time for Kian, Mark and Bryan, who were in the middle of their Leaving Certificate exams. 'It was a strange time,' laughs Bryan, 'it was hard to know which bit was reality.' During this time the boys also started a pre-gig routine that they still stick to today.

'We all come together backstage and talk through the set,' explains Kian. 'Then we just count to three in Irish, say "Westlife", give a big squeeze and say a little prayer. Then me and Shane belly bounce off each other; we go a bit mad backstage!'

Madness aside, Louis decided it was time for the band to showcase for all the major record companies. Obviously no one was going to sign them without seeing the five boys in action. The best way to do that was for IOU to stage a showcase to let people see exactly what they were about. For the showcase, Louis rented the Red Box and invited all the major record companies. Every little detail had been meticulously planned. The Beat gigs had stood the boys in good stead, and they had practised their set over and over until they were word, note and step perfect. The showcase generated an incredible amount of interest. Everyone who saw the boys were impressed by their singing voices and by the way they could fill a stage with personality and entertain just by being them-selves. From that moment there was no doubt that with the right push IOU were certain to be the next big thing to hit Britain. Almost every major record company wanted their signatures on a contract. It was obvious that the five boys were going to be a very big deal indeed.

Among the representatives from the record companies was Simon Cowell, the man who had turned them down when he'd watched them perform at a Dublin hotel. Simon couldn't believe how much the band had changed. Almost from the minute the boys walked out on to the stage he knew he was looking at one of the hottest new acts around. And he wasted no time in telling the boys precisely that. After the showcase he sat down with Kian, Mark, Shane, Bryan and Nicky and told them exactly what RCA could offer them. He told them he'd get them everything they needed to become pop superstars, including the right producers, the right songs and the right stylists. The boys listened carefully to what he was saying and were very impressed with what they heard. More importantly, they liked Simon and trusted what he was telling them. But they were also determined to make their own demands. During the time they'd spent together and through all the recent ups and downs and upheavals, the boys had realized that they had plenty of ideas of their own. They weren't going to be one boy in front and the others in the background. They were going to be full, equal members of a group. IOU had five equal members and they were determined to stay that way. Simon totally agreed. They were also adamant that their fans should see the band as real people. As Bryan explains, 'We're normal blokes. We like to have a few drinks and have a good laugh. We're not going to lie to the fans and tell them we don't have girlfriends and that we don't drink. They have shown us a lot of respect in putting us where we are today through buying our music and supporting us, so I think it would be very disrespectful if we started lying to them.'

Simon had seen what had happened to Take That, who were forced to lead very restrictive lifestyles and were not allowed girlfriends, which was one of the reasons that things fell apart after Robbie Williams left. He agreed wholeheartedly with what the boys were saying. 'He knew exactly what he wanted to do and it sounded fantastic,' remembers Kian. 'We were flying.'

As soon as Simon left the showcase he headed back to London and immediately arranged a meeting with the RCA lawyers. There was no way he was going to let this band slip through his fingers.

# CHAPTER ELEVEN
# SIGNING A RECORD DEAL

Although the boys were in the enviable position of being able to choose which record label they signed with, from the moment they had sat down with Simon there was really no contest. Louis, Ronan and the boys decided to accept the offer from RCA – who had also launched the boy band Take That to pop stardom – which meant they would become the label's pop priority throughout 1999 and the year 2000. The boys began to appreciate the scale of the whole business process as the might of RCA swung into action to groom them into pop superstars. With plenty of time in the public eye ahead each of them needed a new wardrobe. Nothing but the best would do if Shane, Kian, Nicky, Bryan and Mark were to look like pop stars, and soon the boys' wardrobes were full of slick designer labels like Gucci and D&G. Their suits, chosen for them by the Spice Girls' stylist, Kenny Ho, were so sharp that even Boyzone, the pop kings of designer wear, might have been jealous!

'Our clothes are chosen for us,' says Shane, 'but there's no set image. We trust Kenny. He'll come along and ask what we like and the things he picks out for us are usually great. We each have our own individual personality which Kenny tries to reflect in our clothes. He never gets us anything too flashy or too casual.'

Now there was choreography to learn, fitness routines to be stuck to, anything and everything that would give the band an edge over their competition. With everything else in place, it was time to get down to some serious songwriting and recording. And that meant finding some professionals to help them turn what they did naturally into studio magic. Behind the scenes Simon had been busy finding the right songwriters to work with the boys. Songwriting duo Stevie Mac and Wayne Hector were two of the best in the business and they already had a couple of tracks that would be perfect for the boys: 'Swear It Again' and 'Flying Without Wings'. The guys knew the chart potential of the songs as soon as they heard them and couldn't wait to get started on the songs. Even Ronan was impressed by the quality of the songs. 'He told us he wished Boyzone were getting the songs we're getting,' laughs Kian.

Legendary pop producer Max Martin, who had worked with the Backstreet Boys and Five, was also on hand to work with the boys at the Cheiron studios in Sweden. Max was a studio legend, well versed in all the digital tools available and with the knack of coaxing the best performances possible from singers and producers.

▲ The lads do their bit for the Poppy Appeal.

▼ Come on if you think you're hard enough!

(▲) Shane fronts on the Smash Hits tour.

(▼) The boys soak up the well-deserved applause.

▲
Kian looking good
at Party in the Park.

▶

Hunky Kian shows he can sing.

◀ Cheeky but cute —
Shane turns on the charm.

▲ Shane looks the business in his new leather jacket.

Angel-face Nicky used to play for Leeds United.

'Girls like to grab hold of my bum . . .'

▲ Mark looking mischievous at the Nottingham Party in the Park.

◀ Mark turns on the Celtic charm.

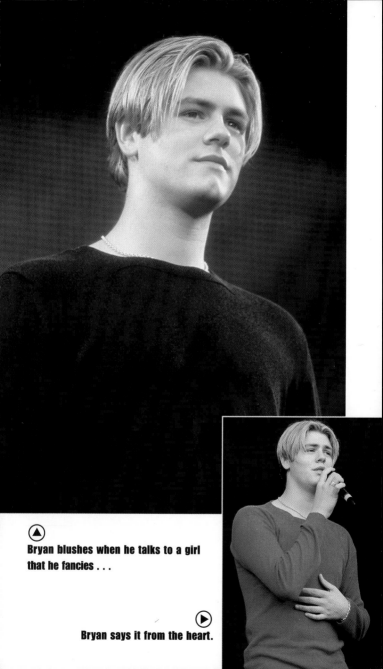

Bryan blushes when he talks to a girl
that he fancies . . .

Bryan says it from the heart.

▲ Gorgeous Mark hits a high note at the TMF Awards . . .

▼ . . . and takes an encore.

There was one remaining thing to change – the band's name. Although IOU was more or less fine for now, something better was needed for when they were ready to catch the public's eye. The boys and their team came up with hundreds of names, but none of them seemed quite right. Then Louis saw the word 'Westside' on a rubbish skip and it struck him that it would be an ideal name for the boys. As soon as Nicky, Shane, Kian, Bryan and Mark heard it they loved it, it just sounded right for them. It was short, it summed up the boys' background, which was exactly what they wanted, and it sounded good. Westside it was to be.

Now that they had their identity, they felt they were poised to take on the world.

# CHAPTER TWELVE
# TOURING WITH BOYZONE

But for now there was just one thing to concentrate on – the boys were due to support Boyzone on their forthcoming tour. Westside spent hours practising their twenty-minute set, which would include the songs 'Everybody Knows', 'If I Let You Go', 'Swear It Again' and 'Flying Without Wings'. There was also choreography to be gone over and over until the five boys could move as one.

The opening night of the Boyzone tour was in Bournemouth. Although the boys had already played to thousands during the Beat gigs, playing at a Boyzone gig was totally different. But they needn't have worried, fans of Boyzone were bound to welcome another Irish boy band, particularly one that was managed by Ronan Keating and looked and sounded as good as Westside. The tours were a huge success, and the boys couldn't believe the positive reaction they got from the crowds. The tour finished with a sold-out gig at Wembley which was a dream come true for the boys. They just hoped that one day they'd be playing there as headliners.

They'd also been given some invaluable advice about touring from the guys in Boyzone. 'They told us to eat properly and things like that,' says Bryan. 'It's very tiring and hard and you have to train a bit because it's exhausting being up early and going to bed late. But it's worth it.'

And Ronan also passed on useful advice on how the boys could improve their performances. 'Ronan would hide under a woolly hat and watch us from the audience and give us tips,' laughs Kian.

During the tour, Shane, Nicky, Bryan, Mark and Kian had got to see a very different side of Ronan, especially since he and fellow Boyzone star Keith Duffy had travelled on the tour bus with them.

'I think they did it just for the craic,' says Nicky. 'It's good to see Ronan let go a bit. He's been famous for so long now that you forget how young he really is. Sometimes he's not the cool pop star at all. He gets really excited about things – just like a kid. I think he missed out on a lot by being famous.'

Keith also shared his memories of starting out in Boyzone with the Westside boys. 'With Keith, we'd be up until four o'clock in the morning having a chat with him,' says Kian. 'He'd tell us loads of old stories about what he was like when he was younger and all that. You really get to know the person and how they dealt with situations that hopefully we'll be in one day.'

Judging from the crowd's reaction there was little doubt that the boys would be every bit as successful as Boyzone. The girls in the audience loved the songs and they loved the boys who sang them even more. It was an amazing reaction, especially as the boys hadn't even done any national press interviews yet. But it didn't take long for the media to catch on. Soon the teen magazines and the national pop columns were tipping Westside as the hottest new band around.

# CHAPTER THIRTEEN
# GETTING DOWN TO WORK

Despite the huge amount of attention surrounding the band there was still a lot of work to be done before they were ready to release their debut single. And the boys were more than ready to get on with it. Touring with a band as big as Boyzone had given Westside something to work towards. Nicky, Shane, Kian, Mark and Bryan were determined to achieve the same level of success as their Irish predecessors. The lads might have gone down a storm with Boyzone fans but if they were to achieve their ultimate ambitions they'd have to establish their own fan base. It followed that a gruelling touring schedule would be required. The venues they were playing were far removed from the glamour of Wembley: instead, the boys played a relentless series of under-18s clubs before joining a BBC roadshow. At times the touring seemed never ending, but they knew that it was essential if they were to find their own fans.

Even more importantly, they needed to prepare for the *Smash Hits* Roadshow in December, where they would be competing against fierce competition from bands like A1 and My Town for the Best New Tour Act award. It was a monotonous and gruelling few months, especially after the excitement of the Boyzone tour, but Anto was on hand to keep the boys motivated when the endless touring seemed too much and to make sure things ran as smoothly as possible. The touring certainly served its purpose and boosted the band's following considerably.

Looking back, this period was a turning point in the boys' careers. Tiring as it was, touring round the country in a cramped people carrier brought the boys closer together, and the gigs had given them the confidence they needed for the *Smash Hits* Roadshow. The Roadshow and The Poll Winners' Party are essential for any new band hoping to make it big. Take That, Boyzone and the Backstreet Boys all got their big breaks in the UK by being voted the Best New Tour Act. If Westside were to achieve the same level of success it was essential that they should follow in their footsteps. The pressure was well and truly on.

But there was no need for anyone to worry: performing was in Westside's blood. Every night they worked their magic on the Roadshow audiences. The response they got was incredible and everyone who saw them at the *Smash Hits* Roadshow couldn't help but fall in love with this new band who looked and sounded like a dream. As soon as the tour was over the boys headed back to Ireland for a well-deserved break. As they walked through Dublin airport looking forward to a few days' rest with their families and friends, Kian's mobile rang. It was the news they had been hoping for: Westside had won the Best New Touring Act award, well ahead of the other bands. Completely forgetting where they were, the boys screamed and hugged each other, jumping up and down with excitement. The world had better get ready: Westside had arrived!

The boys returned to London a few days later for the prestigious *Smash Hits* Poll Winners' Party. As they walked into the famous Docklands arena, the boys couldn't disguise their excitement. A year ago they had watched the show on TV, seeing Five win the award for Best New Tour Act and dreaming that one day it would be them up on that stage. If someone had told them then that the very next year their dream would come true, they would have laughed in disbelief. But amazingly, in just twelve short months everything and more that they had dreamed of had come true. As they walked on stage to collect their golden disc from Boyzone's Stephen Gately, the crowd of fans went wild and the boys couldn't stop smiling. Louis and Ronan were standing out of sight of the TV cameras, clapping and cheering louder than anyone else. As they came off stage the boys gave Louis the trophy to show him just how grateful they were for everything he had done for them. They knew that without their beloved manager they wouldn't have been at the Docklands that day accepting their treasured award.

## CHAPTER FOURTEEN
# A NEW YEAR, A NEW BEGINNING

As 1999 began, Westside had to prove they were worthy of the hype surrounding them. Even though they hadn't even released a single, journalists were clamouring for interviews, trying to find out everything there was to know about the boys, and shows like *Live & Kicking* wanted to book them. Everyone wanted a piece of the Westside action. There was no precedent for this at all. It had never happened quite like this before in the pop world, not even to the Spice Girls, who only sparked Spicemania after the release of their first single, 'Wannabe'. Westside had managed an incredible transition from nobodies to pop's brightest hopes without even releasing a single.

It was time for the boys to show exactly what they were about. The best way to do that was for Westside to arrange a showcase and let people see what they could do.

For the showcase Louis rented the famous Cafe De Paris in London and invited down representatives from the music industry and the UK media. During the run-up to the showcase, Nicky, Shane, Kian, Bryan and Mark were nervous wrecks. They knew that first impressions last, and so were only too aware that their debut official public outing was all-important. Ronan's role as friend and adviser to the band had never been so crucial and he was constantly on hand offering words of wisdom, support and encouragement. The boys hung onto his every word.

'Ronan told us how he and the rest of Boyzone had dealt with similar situations,' says Shane. 'We have learnt so much from his advice. You can't put a price on advice like that. It really is invaluable.'

The boys rehearsed their set over and over until it was absolutely perfect. After all those months touring, the boys' confidence and unity as a band had grown beyond everyone's expectations. Louis and Ronan, as well as the powers that be at RCA, were left in no doubt that the fivesome were ready for what the future held. Confident as they were in their abilities, not even the team who closely watched over Westside's every move could have predicted just how big an impact the five boys were about to make on the pop world.

On Wednesday 3 February – the day of the showcase – Bryan, Nicky, Kian, Mark and Shane waited nervously backstage as the Cafe De Paris began to fill up. Around 200 lucky fans had been invited to attend the showcase to give the venue a feeling of a real gig, and over 300 members of the press and the music business had turned out to see just what all the fuss was about.

The boys knew just how important this showcase was and they were determined to put on the best show of their lives. And they did just that. By the time the lads had sung four songs, screaming fans had proved beyond all doubt that the buzz surrounding Westside was no hype.

Ronan, of course, was there supporting his protégés. 'It was amazing,' he remembers. 'I didn't see the likes of it in the early days of Boyzone. There was many a venue we played around the country where there were more of us on stage than there were people in the audience.'

The atmosphere at the showcase was amazing because it was packed with real fans as well as with the media from the UK and Ireland. For a while it looked as if the hordes of female fans were going to storm the stage to smother the boys wonder.

Instead the fans showed their appreciation by showering the boys with roses and blowing kisses at them. The boys couldn't believe it. 'You should have seen their faces!' laughs Ronan. The fivesome were blown away by all the attention.

Louis was also there, along with Keith from Boyzone. The lads performed several songs, including 'Everybody Knows', 'Flying Without Wings' and 'Swear It Again'. They also impressed the audience when they sang, unaccompanied, a Garth Brooks' song. After the gig everyone was raving about Westside. And not just the fans: the big chiefs from the record company, the editors of *Smash Hits* and the *Live & Kicking* magazine and TV bosses from all the big shows in the UK were knocked out by this sensational boy band. The five boys from Ireland had arrived.

And the story was only just beginning. No sooner had the fivesome finished the showcase than the RCA publicity machine went into overdrive. The demands on the boys' time were constant. It may only have been February but Westside's diary was already full for the next year. Kian, Mark, Shane, Bryan and Mark were busy doing interviews and appearing on television shows. And the UK was just the tip of the iceberg. In the first few months of 1999 they were whisked off to Spain, France, Germany, Switzerland, Norway and Austria. Interest in this new, fantastic-looking boy band was growing rapidly throughout Europe. Gruelling as the boys' agenda was it soon started paying dividends. Television stations, journalists and, most important of all, the fans in Europe were keen to get another chance to see the band. The boys were amazed by the support of their fans and by the reams of fan mail they were beginning to receive.

'The fan mail split is quite even,' says Kian. 'That's something we think is very good for the band, as no one gets jealous.'

'Yeah, it's quite equal,' agrees Nicky. 'It's strange: it changes in different countries, people prefer either Mark or Shane or whoever. It depends on where we go. I'm really popular in Spain!'

'Sadly we didn't get to see much of the countries we visited,' remembers Mark. 'We're a new band just starting off and we have to grab every bit of promotion that we can, so we go from one TV show to another and spend most of our time in cars.'

'We actually get to see very, very few countries,' adds Kian. 'It's normally the airport, taxi and hotel! We do get to see a few places, though. But living out of a suitcase is very tiring.'

'Yeah, it's horrible,' agrees Nicky, 'I hate it, but none of us hate what we're doing because the positives outweigh the negatives. We're very lucky people, some of the luckiest in the whole world.'

It was now time to get down to some serious song-writing and recording, and to turn the magic the boys performed on stage into hit singles. The fivesome climbed onto a plane and headed to Stockholm, where the Cheiron Studios are based. The studio looks run-down from the outside, a ten-minute drive away from the centre of Stockholm, but inside it's state-of-the-art and has been used by many big names in the music business including the Backstreet Boys, 'N Sync and Five. Once inside the studio, it was time for the boys to take the plunge, to use all that Louis and Ronan had taught them as well as everything they'd since worked out for themselves. This was for real. This was where the Westside adventure really began and the boys were ready to rock the world.

Although the pressure was on – studio time is very expensive – the boys had fun recording. Yes, it was serious business, requiring long, often monotonous, hours of work, but they loved every moment of it. And whenever they got a break, the five lads would run up the rickety staircase that lead to the basement studio and burst out of the building into the winter snow that blanketed the building to engage in some pretty fierce snowball fights.

When the recording was complete, the boys returned home – with a new name. There had been a problem registering 'Westside' in America as someone was already using it. It was a blow for the boys: they liked Westside, it just sounded right for them. A complete name change would have been costly for the record company and, anyway, the boys had already won their award at the *Smash Hits* Poll Winners' Party as Westside and they didn't want to confuse their fans.

'We didn't want the name to change too much,' confirms Kian. 'We wanted to change just a bit of the name – it had to be West-something because we wanted to still keep the fact that we're from the west of Ireland and the west of Europe.'

So it was decided that with just a little alteration they could still make it work. If they couldn't be Westside, then they'd be Westlife. They all loved it. It was perfect. Next stop: the top of the world!

# CHAPTER FIFTEEN
# SWEAR IT AGAIN

It was time for the re-christened Westlife to prepare for the release of their first single, 'Swear It Again'. It had been decided that the single should be released in Ireland on 29 March, then in the UK two weeks later. The pressure was well and truly on, especially as the single was being released after seven months of hype. Kian, Bryan, Mark, Nicky and Shane were acutely aware that they had a lot to live up to. What would happen if the single bombed? As it happened, the boys didn't have time to sit and worry about it as they immediately embarked on a promotional tour of Ireland, appearing on radio shows and at signing sessions in HMV stores. Everyone who came into contact with the boys or saw them on TV was overwhelmed by their sense of fun and down-to-earth honesty. These were five polite, charming boys who had not let the overwhelming events of the last few months go to their heads – and who looked like they were having the time of their lives.

Of course, they didn't gain universal approval – no one ever does. Some members of the media were all too ready to knock the idea of yet another boy band and Nicky, Mark, Shane, Bryan and Kian were asked over and over again whether there was room for another boy band in the pop business. The boys would wearily rub their faces and smile politely as Shane answered time after time, 'No one ever says "do we need another rock band or female singer"... Why do they single out boy bands? Besides, we prefer to think of ourselves as a pop group.'

A week later, everyone's faith in Westlife was proved founded when 'Swear It Again' rocketed into the Irish charts at number one. But the nail-biting wait wasn't over. Would the single do as well in the UK? The answer was an unequivocal 'Yes'. As soon as the single hit the shops it started selling. Westlife were hot. The song was so full of hooks, it couldn't fail to catch the attention of anyone listening. Westlife all waited nervously for the UK charts to come out. The lads had all been up early as they were unable to sleep. The good news was that they'd be put out of their misery by about 12.30, which was when they'd hear whether 'Swear It Again' had got to number one or not.

'Swear It Again' was certainly up against some heavy competition: Fatboy Slim was in the running with 'Right Here, Right Now' and Texas was also being tipped for the top. Of course, the lads would have dearly loved to have a number one at this point in their careers. Thanks to the mid-week charts, they knew they were definitely going to be in the top three, which was a major achievement for a new band's debut single. It had already been an amazing week for Westlife. They'd flown to Boston to showcase for record company bosses from all around the world. They had chosen to perform live and their energy had blown everyone away. All the record companies around the world now wanted a piece of the action.

Two days later the fivesome were back in London to record *Top Of The Pops*. *TOTP* is recorded on a Thursday and then it goes out on Friday evenings. The band literally spent one day and night at the big record company conference in Boston and then hopped on a plane and hightailed it back to London to realize a dream – appearing on *Top Of The Pops*. As Kian put it, 'I never thought I'd see the day that I flew to America just for one day and night. But as Ronan says that's the way it is in this business.'

There are TV shows and there are TV shows, but *Top Of The Pops* is very special. It has hosted virtually every great name in pop music since it first aired in 1964. From the Beatles to Madonna, it's every band's greatest wish to appear on the show. It's really a legendary TV pop show, and every would-be pop star has grown up dreaming of the day they'll appear on the show; now that dream was coming true for Westlife.

They may have been jet-lagged after getting off a plane from the States, but the Westlife lads were in top form as they made their way to the studio. The boys were in constant contact with Ronan, busy rehearsing with Boyzone, who gave them much-needed encouragement and advice.

'I wanted to make sure that they were relaxed and confident and knew exactly what to expect,' explains Ronan. 'I did tell them to enjoy the experience, but also to treat it with respect because it's not every pop band that makes it all the way to *Top Of The Pops*.'

True enough, and Westlife had done it with their first single. There are other bands out there who would give anything to have that opportunity. The boys knew just how lucky they were, and they were determined to keep their feet on the ground and not let their instant success go to their heads.

There were 200 young fans waiting outside the *Top Of The Pops* studio in Shepherd's Bush, west London, when the boys arrived. Nicky, Bryan, Mark, Shane and Kian went over to them and signed as many autographs as they could before going in to rehearse. Later on they came out again to meet the fans – after all, it's the fans who have put them where they are today.

Going in to the *Top Of The Pops* studio was a moment to savour for Westlife. Of course they'd seen it on TV, but they were surprised at how small it seemed. Nevertheless, for them, the studio had a definite magic; it was amazing. There are five stages and they couldn't get over seeing all the other performers wandering along the corridors.

'We saw Texas and Suede, and Martine McCutcheon came over to wish us the best of luck with our careers,' remembers Kian. 'It was a wonderful experience for all of us, something we'll treasure for the rest of our lives.'

And everyone who caught their debut appearance on *Top Of The Pops* will certainly remember Westlife. The boys were obviously overjoyed to be there and, as ever, gave their performance everything.

Now they had to keep their fingers crossed for the UK chart. Just before 12.30, the news came through: 'Swear It Again' was number one with a bullet! The boys were on top of the world. Of course they had dreamt about having a number one smash hit since they got together, but having all their fantasies come true so dramatically was a different matter. They were number one! Needless to say, RCA were more than pleased. Their faith in the band had been amply rewarded.

Now questions were buzzing around the Westlife camp. What song would they release next? Would it be like the first single? And, most importantly, would it be a smash hit? The last question seemed to have a pretty obvious answer. No group was going to have such a large impact and then simply disappear. Westlife were going to be around for a long while.

# CHAPTER SIXTEEN
# IF I LET YOU GO

On 4 July, Westlife made their way to Hyde Park to take part in one of the biggest music concerts of the year. The Party In The Park drew a crowd of more than 100,000 fans to watch their favourite acts, including the Corrs, Geri Halliwell and Steps, perform for the Prince's Trust. And this year, Westlife were sharing the stage. It was hard to believe that exactly a year earlier, the final line-up of Westlife had been decided and the boys' heads had been full of hopes and dreams that now, just twelve months later, were coming true. The boys would also be performing their new single, 'If I Let You Go'. Once again the pressure was on: everyone wanted to know whether or not Westlife could repeat 'Swear It Again''s success. Hitting the top first time round was remarkable enough. Twice in succession would be incredible.

People didn't have to wait long to find out whether Westlife were in the running for a second chart-topper. 'If I Let You Go' was released on 9 August, but even before the single reached the stores, it was a massive, sure-fire hit. Ronan, who was at number one with his solo hit, 'When You Say Nothing At All', taken from the soundtrack of the film *Notting Hill*, was left facing a rather uncomfortable situation.

'It's going to be a close call in the charts,' he said. 'The lads of Westlife are expecting a number one for their single, and mine's at number one. It's a strange position for me to be in, because obviously I want my first solo single to do well for as long as possible. But at the same time, I want Westlife to do well.'

Sure enough, 'If I Let You Go' rocketed straight into the chart at number one, knocking Ronan off the top spot. And that made Westlife the first boy band ever to go straight to number one with their first two singles. Now nobody could doubt that this group were the biggest thing to hit music in years.

The video that accompanied the song had been filmed in the dramatic surroundings of Tenerife in the Canary Islands and remains the boys' favourite to date. It's not surprising really: they got to stay in the luxury of the exclusive Hotel Mencey in the city of Santa Crux de Tenerife. They had the time of their lives as they travelled around the beautiful island in a people carrier. In between filming, they visited the volcano El Teide in Las Canadas Del Teide International Park, where they got rather badly burnt in the scorching sun. Then they moved on to Playa del Boyullo, a beach on the west side of the island, where they met up with the army of extras who also appeared in the video. For once the boys didn't mind the tedious waiting around that goes hand in hand with making a video, as it meant they had plenty of time to muck around in the sun-warmed water or to just laze on the beach listening to Mariah Carey and the Backstreet Boys on their Walkmans and chatting to friends on their mobile phones. So it's no wonder that the video shows the boys at their most relaxed as they stroll along the shore – they really were having a fantastic time and the video was a great accompaniment to the song.

A video is a standard industry way to sell a single, but by now it was debatable whether Westlife even needed one. A few still pictures to accompany the song would probably have done the trick just as well.

By then, though, the chart position of the song almost didn't matter. Even though they'd released only two singles, no one in pop music had had a bigger year than Westlife. No other boy band, not even Take That, arguably the biggest boy band of all time, had gone straight to number one with their first two singles. Who could say what Westlife would achieve before it was over?

Still, none of the boys had expected all of this to happen. No one, even in their wildest dreams, could have imagined how big Westlife would become. Certainly the pop business was being very good to them, but it showed just what you achieve if you are willing to give everything you've got got something and push to win.

Their third single, 'Flying Without Wings' was released on 28 October and zoomed straight to the top of the charts, just as their previous two singles had. 'There has been a fair bit of pressure on us because of our first two singles,' admitted Mark. 'We're just overjoyed that we have got a third number one. It's just amazing.' To commemorate their success, and the fact that they were already making a big name for themselves in the pop record books, the boys went out for a celebratory meal and drinks with their friends.

At the beginning of November, just in time to be on everyone's Christmas list, the album *Westlife* was released. It was probably the most anticipated record of the year. The sales of the singles had been exceptional, but *Westlife* was vanishing from the stores as quickly as staff could put it on the shelves. There was little competition and the album rocketed straight to number two.

'It's all happening so fast,' said Nicky, reflecting on the Westlife whirlwind. 'One day we were no one, the next our single's number one. It really is amazing.'

# CHAPTER SEVENTEEN
# WESTLIFE:
## THE ALBUM

There's no two ways about it, the whole of *Westlife* is about love. How it makes the world go round; how it can leave you with a broken heart; how it can be heaven and can be hell. On *Westlife*, the boys explore the very different avenues that love can take, and in the process they have created a pop masterpiece.

The album opens with their first number one hit, 'Swear It Again', in which the boys pledge their love to that special someone. The piano-driven ballad is all about the promises that true love brings and makes the listener want to reach out and draw that special person even closer. It's the kind of song Elton John would surely kill for; a hit from start to finish.

The second track on the album is the second single, 'If I Let You Go', which is all about loving someone but being scared to let them know how you feel. As the boys open up their hearts, the song talks about the pain that being in love can bring. It's a little bit more up-tempo and features a more shuffling beat than

'Swear It Again', but both songs have the same soul-stirring magic.

The third track is the third single, 'Flying Without Wings'. This is a classic ballad in which sweeping strings accompany the heartfelt lyrics and the angelic voices of the boys. It's uplifting yet full of tenderness, and is definitely one for the grown-ups.

Then comes 'Fool Again', which is all about a girl leaving a relationship behind her, while the boys sing the part of her devastated boyfriend, unable to believe that he may just have lost the love of his life. The love affair might have ended but there are still lots of questions about where it all went wrong. Alluring harmonies complement the song's beautiful melody.

Next on the album is 'No No', a track which gives Westlife the chance to go groovy; this one was made for dancing around the bedroom to. The lyrics pledge devotion, and are set to an upbeat melody. Pure pop at its very best.

The next track on the album is 'I Don't Wanna Fight'. It's a classical song about heartbreak. The boys are nursing broken hearts and deliver the message of the song with a pained passion: life's too short for fussing and fighting and unless the people in the song can get past the constant arguments, there won't be any relationship worth fighting for. Perhaps it's a message that everyone should learn from.

Next up is 'Change The World' – another song about the ending of a relationship and the lengths the boys are prepared to go to, if it means they could win back the love they have lost. It's a mid-tempo number with superb vocal performances by all the boys, show-casing the full range of their vocal talent.

The eighth track on the album is 'Moments', another heartfelt ballad, this time it's about the wonder of falling in love. The magic of spending time with that very special someone is exquisitely captured in this spine-tingling love song.

Then comes 'Seasons In The Sun' – a distinctively Irish treatment of the classic song that was a number one hit for folk singer, Terry Jacks, way back in 1974. Anyone who has heard this version will be hoping that the boys release it as a single. Let's hope they do, and make the heartbreakingly innocent song about the dying words of a young man injured in war a chart-topper for the millennium.

The tenth track is 'I Need You'. Here the boys sing about a relationship in which they've been unfaithful, but the message is that they have learnt from their mistake and are promising that they will be 100 per cent true from now on. It's upbeat and groovy, with the dancey rhythm contrasting with the sad sentiment of the song.

Then comes 'Miss You'. The clever change of rhythm makes this one of the most outstanding tracks on the album. Celtic sounds mixed with a guitar-based rhythm give the song a truly distinctive sound.

Next is 'More Than Words'. This is a cover of the hit song by the US male vocal and instrumental group Extreme, which reached number two in the charts in 1991, staying in the charts for 11 weeks. The boys take an already fantastic song, add their own special rhythm and Irish charm, and come up with a winner for a whole new audience.

'Open Your Heart' is a great showcase for the boys' intricate harmonies. The rhythm slowly builds through the beginning of the song and gets funkier about halfway through, as the boys plead for that special girl to give them a second chance. How could she resist?

Then comes 'Try Again'. The signature Celtic sound of Westlife is in full effect throughout this sweet ballad. Love may have ended but there are no hard feelings, only a message of hope that the girl who has been left behind will find love again, however she feels right now.

'What I Want Is What I've Got' is definitely the most funky song on the album. It's a celebration of discovering true love and a great excuse to grab that boy of your dreams, hold him close and never let him go.

On 'We Are One', Westlife do Andrew Lloyd Webber. It's a song that would be perfect for any film soundtrack; a great song to lie in bed and listen to last thing at night.

The closing song on the album is 'Can't Lose What You Never Had' and it is without a doubt the sexiest song on *Westlife*. The boys advocate grabbing the opportunity with both hands if you're lucky enough to see that special person, because you can't lose what you never had. The sultry rhythms of this track combine with the boys' compelling vocals to make a song that will instantly seduce anyone who listens to it. A perfect end to a perfect album.

# CHAPTER EIGHTEEN
# WESTLIFE AND LOVE

Judging by their songs, the Westlife boys certainly know a thing or two about love. There have been rumours linking different members of Westlife with everyone from Mariah Carey to Britney Spears. So what's the real story?

Nicky is the only member of Westlife who isn't single. He's been dating his girlfriend, Georgina, for five years and is very much in love. The couple met at school, and for Nicky it was love at first sight. 'She was sitting at the front of the classroom and I liked her immediately. She is very pretty, has beautiful eyes and there was just something about her.'

That night Nicky went home from school and told his mum that he'd met the girl of his dreams. However, the course of true love didn't run smoothly at the beginning. Nicky was too shy to talk to Georgina so he contented himself with going out of his way to pass her in the school corridor and flashing her a quick smile. It was two years before he had the courage to do anything about it and even then he got his friend to ask her out for him. Georgina said 'no'. Nicky was devastated but determined not to give up.

A year later he got another friend to ask her out for him and this time Georgina said 'yes'. They went to a party together the night before Nicky's sixteenth party but didn't start seeing each other properly for a few months. They've been together ever since.

'She's stuck by me through thick and thin,' says Nicky, proudly. 'I've loved her since the first moment I saw her and I owe her so much.'

Georgina's dad is the Prime Minister of Ireland, which makes for some unconventional domestic arrangements. 'It's odd when we join him for Sunday lunch and there are four or five policemen around all the time. That's kind of scary,' Nicky laughs. 'But if I'm just out with Georgina on my own, then we're not under surveillance because she tries to lead as normal a life as possible. After all, it's not her that's Prime Minister, it's her dad.'

The Prime Minister, though, has taken a great interest in Westlife, and makes a point of mentioning the band in interviews on radio and TV.

'He's been really supportive,' says Mark. 'When we launched "Swear It Again" in Ireland he came along and sat in the middle of the balcony of the place we were playing. Suddenly I looked up and there was the Prime Minister bopping away. I couldn't stop laughing.'

The other Westlife boys are happy being single but are open to some romance, especially after seeing just how good a relationship Nicky has with Georgina. 'She's always the person who shows me the light at the end of the tunnel and she always sees the positive side. I need to have someone who's there for me,' Nicky confesses.

'To get a solid foundation is difficult,' acknowledges Shane. 'I'm just so jealous of Nicky – he and Georgina have such a solid basis because they've been dating for so long. Everything has become harder for us with relationships since we've been in the band. It's difficult to keep in touch, especially when we're touring, but it is still possible to go out with girls. It's just a matter of finding the right one.'

'It's hard, lonely and sad,' admits Kian. 'I've got a reputation as a bit of a womanizer, but it's not true. I get on with girls but that's as far as it goes. I'm a hopeless romantic and I can't wait until I meet the right girl for me.'

'Yeah,' sighs Bryan, 'I would love to have a relationship, but I want to be totally sure if a girl likes me for my personality or for my image in the band.'

Mark is quite content to be single at the moment. 'I'm too young,' he says, 'there's plenty of time for all that. Being in the band has made me more cautious about meeting girls: I want them to be interested in me, not the band.'

They've got nothing to worry about in the love stakes. With the kind of looks and personality that all five members of Westlife have, it can only be a matter of time before each of them finds the girl of his dreams.

## A SPOTLIGHT ON WESTLIFE IN LOVE

### How would a girl get you to go out with her?

**Mark** She'd have to be really funny and a good laugh.

**Bryan** Just by smiling at me, because I've never been chatted up before!

**Nicky** Eye contact for me, definitely.

**Kian** Just by being a nice person – by being herself.

**Shane** She'd need to be presentable so that I liked her at first glance.

**Bryan** I'm not into made-up, fake-looking girls. I prefer someone natural and different looking.

### What kind of girl do you go for?

**Mark** I like different sorts of girls. You kind of know when you see someone that you could get on with.

**Nicky** Very ladylike and smart, not steely looking.

**Kian** Natural looking with something different about her.

**Shane** Very well-presented but not too much make-up. I don't like girls who look like they've taken hours to get ready.

### How would she catch your eye?

**Mark** Well, to start with, if she was nice-looking and she had nice clothes on, I'd notice her. But I'd have to see what she was like as a person.

**Bryan** I always notice a smile first.

**Nicky** By looking at me!

**Kian** If she was good-looking she'd catch my eye anyway!

**Shane** A nice smile would do it every time.

## How would you approach her, or would you prefer her to approach you?

**Mark** I'd walk over with my friend and we'd ease our way into the conversation.

**Bryan** I wouldn't do either. I'd wait for us to bump into each other.

**Nicky** I'd wait and see if she approached me – if she didn't, I'd go over to her.

**Kian** If I was getting signals off her but it looked like she was too shy to come over, I'd approach her.

**Shane** If I really liked her I'd go over, or 'accidentally' bump into her.

## What should be her opening line?

**Mark** 'How's it going? Are you having a good night?' I wouldn't like her to say she liked my single or anything like that!

**Bryan** I'd like her to ask me out for a drink. That would be perfect.

**Nicky** Something funny and nothing to do with the band!

**Kian** Something casual. No terrible chat-up lines, they're not necessary!

**Shane** Something short and sweet, so you want to know more!

## What should she be wearing?

**Mark** Well, I really like Mel C's style, but then again I think Mariah Carey looks really good. I basically like all kinds of clothes.

**Bryan** I do like short skirts and I like smart girls.

**Nicky** Like I said, classy.

**Kian** I like the baggy trousers and sneakers look, but I also like slick girls. Anything!

**Shane** Some girls look gorgeous in combats and some look gorgeous in hipsters, so whatever they look gorgeous in!

## What perfume should she wear?

**Mark** Most girls smell nice anyway, so that's enough for me!

**Bryan** Tommy Girl.

**Nicky** Eternity by Calvin Klein, definitely.

**Kian** I love White Musk.

**Shane** Cool Water for Women.

## What should her hair be like?

**Mark** I don't mind as long as she's nice-looking!

**Bryan** I like either a girl with blonde hair, or a girl with jet-black hair. Extremes are good.

**Kian** Blonde, dark, red, short, long, up, down, whatever.

**Shane** Natural – I'm not mad keen on blue hair!

## Would you like her to look like anyone famous?

**Mark** Mariah Carey. I think she's beautiful.

**Bryan** Jennifer Love Hewitt.

**Nicky** Nope, just herself.

**Kian** Anybody, ha, ha, ha!

**Shane** I think Nicole Kidman, Catherine Zeta Jones and Cameron Diaz are beautiful.

## What would really put you off a girl?

**Mark** If she was picking her nose or had smelly breath. Yeuch!

**Bryan** If she was arrogant and big-headed.

**Nicky** If she was too forward.

**Kian** Someone saying, 'I fancy you because you're Kian from Westlife.' A big no-no.

**Shane** If a girl came up to me and started telling me her life story. Or if she had bad breath.

## Have you ever had a nightmare girl experience?

**Mark** Once, some of my friends told this girl that I liked her, so she started chatting me up. I felt really awful and all my mates sat giggling in the corner.

**Bryan** Yes, I was grabbed a few times by drunk girls when I worked on security in McDonald's. That was a total nightmare.

**Kian** I've been sent some very weird, very pervy letters.

**Shane** I've had girls I've chatted up turning into complete psychos and decide that we should spend our lives together. Scary!

## Which *Friends* girl?

**Mark** Monica

**Bryan** Rachel

**Nicky** Monica

**Kian** Rachel

**Shane** Phoebe

## Which Steps girl?
**Mark** Lisa
**Bryan** Claire
**Nicky** All of them!
**Kian** Lisa
**Shane** Faye

## Which All Saint?
**Mark** Shaznay or Nic
**Bryan** Nic
**Nicky** Nic
**Kian** Nic
**Shane** Nat

## Which B*Witched babe?
**Mark** Lindsay
**Bryan** Sinead
**Nicky** All of them!
**Kian** Lindsay
**Shane** Lindsay

## Which Spice Girl?
**Mark** Victoria
**Bryan** Mel C
**Nicky** Victoria
**Kian** Emma
**Shane** Victoria

**Do you have loads of girls screaming for you wherever you go these days?**

**Kian** We always get loads of girls waiting for us at the airport in Ireland, and even before we had our single out over there, we had to have security as soon as we landed.

**Are you always faithful in a relationship?**

**Bryan** I think it depends how much you like your girl-friend, really. If it's only a new thing and then you meet someone you prefer, you obviously do some-thing about it rather than let the opportunity pass. It's different if it's a serious relationship.

**Do you get embarrassed snogging in public?**

**Shane** I did used to get embarrassed when I was about 14. But now? I don't think so...

**Do you think you'd make a really good boyfriend?**

**Kian** I like to think I would, but I don't really know. I've been out with a lot of girls before and I like to treat them well, you know, take them out to movies and to dinner on Valentine's Day... stuff like that.

**If money was no object, where would you take a girl to impress her?**

**Nicky** Let's see... I know – I'd take her to Paris, Sydney, the USA, everywhere! We could go round the world on a yacht and we'd drink the finest champagne and watch the sun set. I'd make sure she had a good time, y'know?

### Do you think you'll get married one day?

**Mark** I've no plans whatsoever to get married. You know I'm still really young, so commitment and all that stuff is out the window until I'm in my thirties or forties. It's the Nineties after all – people are getting married when they're 65! Whenever the time is right, I'll do it.

### When was the last time you told someone you loved them?

**Mark** The last person I said 'I love you' to was my mother. I'm very close to everyone back home in Sligo.

### Do you get lonely when you're not going out with someone?

**Kian** Yeah, I'd love to have a girlfriend, 'cos I get very lonely being away from home. I think about girls every minute of the day!

### Who's the best at chatting up the laydeez?

**Bryan** Kian. He changes his personality depending on who he's talking to. When he's chatting up a girl, he's different from when he's with us. He's smooth.

### How do you know when you've fallen in love?

**Mark** Love is when you would do absolutely anything for that person. If you love someone, and they said one thing and a thousand people said the opposite, you'd still be on their side, you'd be behind them all the way. I think the worst thing ever would be to be in love with someone and not be loved back by them.

## What's the best way to say 'I love you'?

**Nicky** It's a very important statement which should only be made when you're alone. Over dinner would be nice.

# CHAPTER NINETEEN
# SO WHAT NOW?

As 1999 draws to a close, Westlife have been busy reflecting on what they have achieved so far in their short career. None of them could have envisaged how much their lives would change in such a short time. They've done it... and done it, and done it again. Despite their whirlwind success, the boys have managed to keep their egos and their sense of humour in check. It would have been so easy for their heads to become inflated. It's no longer possible for the five lads to lead a 'real' life, what with the demands on their waking hours, plane trips across continents and round after round of interviews. But they've managed to embrace all the hard work with good grace and retain a sense of fun to overcome the endless hours of travel.

'Our lives have totally changed,' admits Shane. 'We're suddenly flying all over the world going to different countries. Sometimes we've been to four different countries in one day: we've woken up in Sweden, had breakfast in Denmark, done a TV show in Germany and gone to bed in Holland.'

'Yeah,' laughs Kian. 'We have to ring our mums to check what day it is.'

The pressure is stronger than ever to keep succeeding. The five lads have no time to themselves. For the moment, they don't mind: they can take it all in their stride.

They owe a lot of their healthy approach to pop stardom to Ronan and the other Boyzone boys, who have become close friends as well as mentors. Westlife have seen the way that Boyzone have dealt with the trappings of fame and have learnt from their experiences, both good and bad. One of the most memorable times for them was when Stephen Gately came out.

'When Stephen knew the story about him being gay was going to be in the papers you could see he was very nervous and concerned about the reaction he'd get from the fans,' remembers Bryan. 'But as soon as it appeared in the press, the public's response was amazing. It blew him away when fans turned up with banners saying they still loved him.'

'Stephen said that it felt like the sun opened up above him and he was on a high for the rest of the tour. He's a lovely guy and a great friend of ours,' adds Nicky. 'It's good to see him so happy.'

Once they're fully established with a substantial body of work behind them, Westlife will be able to settle down a little, to relax. The pressure will ease. For now, though, being a pop band at the forefront on the industy means that they constantly have to keep proving themselves. They're blazing a trail, not only for themselves, but for all the bands that will undoubtedly follow them.

So what might the future really hold for Westlife?

There's talk of a Westlife film, with Ronan making a cameo appearance as himself. And no doubt somewhere in the years ahead all five boys may fall in love and get married, although they have a gentleman's agreement with Louis not to marry for Westlife's first five years.

'Louis said at the start, "I hope none of you is going to get married and have babies",' says Bryan. 'We said "of course we're not". If someone meets someone they love and wants to get married and have kids, they are still free to do that. But we've agreed among ourselves that it would be stupid at this stage. If you got married now, it would affect your career, because you're going to be so focused on your family and your wife. I think it's just a bit silly.'

But as was the case with Boyzone, if those events do happen they won't break up the group; they've been through so much already. The boys have such a groundswell of support, which is growing all the time, that it would be impossible for them to disappear from the scene overnight. In all likelihood, over the next few years the boys will experience remarkable growth, both artistically and personally.

'You can succeed with whatever you're happy with,' says Shane. 'Never worry about things too much unless you have to.'

For a supposedly manufactured boy band, Westlife have broken out of any mould that could have cramped or altered them, and have become an even bigger sensation because of it. They've shown that you can realize your heart's desires. They've given us everything and they won't stop for a very long time.

# CHAPTER TWENTY
# THE WEIRD AND WONDERFUL WORLD OF WESTLIFE

### Bryan made Ronan's mate puke!

We were round at Ronan's having dinner. One of his friends was having a drink and we swapped his short with a swig of vinegar. Then we started going, 'Drink, drink, drink!' He did it, his face turned green and then he puked everywhere!

### Mark dressed up as a posh laydee!

When I was in the Scouts we put on a play and I had to dress up as a woman! I was in a small scene with another guy – he was dressed up as a sporty woman and I was working a posh look. I was wearing a scarf, my mum's high heels, earrings, a skirt and Mum's big coat from about twenty years ago. It was in front of my whole parish – can you imagine how embarrassing that was?

### Kian's life was saved by a washing line!

I was in a holiday centre where this event called the Community Games was taking place. It must have been around midnight and I was sitting on this railing out on a balcony that was a bit wet. Next thing you know, my foot slipped and I fell back. Luckily enough my foot got caught in a clothes line which broke my fall. I fell headfirst about two storeys and I was knocked unconscious with a dislocated shoulder. Who knows what would have happened without that washing line!

### Nicky once pretended to be a member of OTT!

I must have been about 17 and I was living in Leeds. Me and three other lads from Dublin got chatting to these girls who asked us what we were doing in England. So we told them we were in a new Irish band called OTT, 'cos it was around the time when OTT were about to hit Britain. And they believed us! They asked us if we knew Boyzone and we pretended we did. They even asked us for our autographs! In a way it wasn't so much a lie as a premonition, 'cos three years later I am in a boy band and I do know Boyzone!

### Mark was weed on!

My auntie had a newborn kitten and it was so gorgeous I was cuddling it and I wouldn't let it go. Next thing I knew it had weed all over my smart top that I was wearing to go out for lunch.

### Kian torments Nicky about his phobias!

Nicky's terrified about being stuck in a lift, so I'm always dragging him into them, jumping up and down, pretending it's stuck, anything just to freak him out! Actually, I torment Nicky about most of his phobias.

### Bryan was once a self-confessed geek!

I collected *Discovery* magazine. Looking back it was such a boring thing to do 'cos it's all about stuff like the Kings and Queens of England. I used to keep each copy carefully stashed away in a file.

### Nicky snogged eleven girls in one night!

It was at a party to celebrate our exam results and I must have been about 15. It's one of those nights when everyone goes out and goes mad. I was at this nightclub called The Furnace in Dublin, which has actually closed down now!

### Shane wears dirty knickers!

I went away for a three-day rugby tournament and I forgot all about my boxer shorts. We were in the middle of nowhere and I had to wear the same pair day in, day out, even during the matches. They smelt after a while!

### Mark was told off by a girlfriend's parents!

I was meeting my girlfriend's parents for the first time and I was trying to sound like the nicest little kid ever. They asked me about my interests and I said, 'I like singing, dancing and go-karting.' Their faces dropped and I got a huge lecture about the dangers of go-karting and was warned never to take their daughter near a go-kart. It was so embarrassing!

### Shane used to flash on the beach!

When I was younger I was always getting caught changing on the beach. Usually I'd be spotted in the sand dunes with my wet shorts half on and half off. I'd think, 'Great! No one can see me here', and then a group of girls would come past and see the lot.

### Bryan once peed on his auntie's face!

I was only a baby at the time. She was changing my nappy and I peed a direct hit in her face. She loves telling that story in front of my friends!

### Nicky's mum dressed him up as a girl!

My mum always used to dress me up the same as my sister until I was about six. Not exactly the same, but if my sister had a pink tracksuit I'd have the same tracksuit in blue and there are loads of pictures of us wearing the same T-shirts and shorts. Really nice...

### Bryan was a very bad person!

All my aunties hated me as a child and they refused to look after me. I used to put bleach in the milk bottles and I once flushed my mum's wedding rings down the toilet. She never found them again! I also cut my own hair the day before Communion because I had a horrible bowl 'do which swept to the side. My mum wasn't happy.

### Shane snogged his girlfriend's mates!

Loads of 'em! When I was about 14 if I was with just one girl I'd always end up with three or four of her friends, one after the other. In fact, I went out with one girl just because I fancied her best friend. It was the easiest way to get near her!

### Kian's a serial window-smasher!

I broke my neighbour's window twice, once with a water bomb and then a snowball. They were both accidental, but I didn't feel bad 'cos she always used to take my football away from me. She came up to my mother the other day and said, "Oh Kian, he's doing great isn't he?" so I don't think there are any hard feelings.

### Nicky was the headmaster's pet!

My headmaster was a football manager, so he absolutely loved me! I remember when Georgina and I first started going out we were caught snogging at the school gates. Anyway, the next day she was hauled in front of him and I wasn't.

### Bryan was punished for his loud farts!

When I was at school I got lines for dropping a big, squelchy loud fart. My teacher, who was a priest, made me write 'I must not fart in class' one hundred times. I left that school shortly afterwards.

### Shane played with girls' toys!

I used to have a toy cat called Kitty. It wasn't a pink cat but it wasn't a black cat either, if you know what I mean. It was something a girl would definitely have had. I'd hide him under my bed when my friends came around.

### Bryan peed in public!

I'd always be doing it just when loads of people were walking past and my pee was trickling down the lane. They'd have to jump over it to avoid stepping in it.

### Kian blubbed in a club!

When I broke up with my first serious girlfriend I was absolutely gutted. One night I was in this club and of course my ex-girlfriend was there. And after a few drinks I got a little emotional and I ended up just slumped in a corner crying my eyes out all night!

### Kian dressed up as Marilyn Monroe!

It was for a musical variety show and I sang 'Happy Birthday'. I also dressed up as Cilla Black, and I have to say I was good at both of them. I had two big balloons up my dress, a blonde wig and a beauty spot and I hitched the dress up so you could see my boxer shorts underneath.

### Nicky stole from his best friend!

I've never admitted this to anyone before but when I was in primary school the circus came to town and everyone in the class got a ticket each, but I wanted an extra one. I remember watching my best friend, Colm, putting his ticket in his pencil case and it was too tempting, so I stole it! I've never told him to this day. Sorry, Colm!

### Bryan wears girls' bra tops!

There's a photo of me on holiday a few years ago wearing a pair of my jeans and my sister's tiny pink bra top. I had my hair up and sunglasses on my head. I did it for a laugh and my sister still keeps the picture on her wall.

## Mark snogged two cousins in one night!

One Halloween night my mates and I got talking to this group of girls and we all snogged one of the girls. Then we went off and we bumped into another group of girls and I snogged this girl who I later found out was the first girl's cousin! Then we went on to a night-club and I snogged another girl – she wasn't connected, thank goodness!

## Shane was very familiar with ladies' lingerie!

I used to flick straight to the lingerie section in my mum's catalogues. I thought it was deadly. That was my first glimpse of real women! I remember one day watching a girl in her bedroom just as she started undoing her trousers. The window sill got in the way so I couldn't see anything. Then she was just about to pull her top off but she changed her mind and pulled the blind down!

## Kian's a motorway mooner!

When I was on football trips, we'd be travelling in the bus and the whole team would moon all the cars behind us. We'd all just stick our cheeks to the window! No one ever seemed very impressed!

### Nicky once appeared on TV with no pants on!

It was a TV show in Italy and basically me, Shane, Bryan and Kian did a performance with no boxer shorts on. We let it all hang loose! We were wearing white trousers and Shane had black boxers on which were showing through. So he couldn't wear them and the rest of us decided to keep him company!

### Bryan and Kian share girls!

Me and Kian always used to compete for girls and since we've been in the band there's been about six or seven girls that both of us have gone out with. It back-fired on us once though, when it turned out we were seeing the same girl at the same time without realizing it.

### Bryan can spit a long way!

I bite my fingernails and spit them out. I once spat off a roof and hit someone. I didn't mean to, but it was a direct hit!

# CHAPTER TWENTY-ONE
# THE ULTIMATE WESTLIFE QUIZ

1) Which member of Westlife once dressed up as Marilyn Monroe?

2) Why was Bryan teased at school?

3) Why was Nicky released from his football contract at Leeds United?

4) Where did the band's previous name, Westside, come from?

5) Who is Nicky's girlfriend's father?

6) How did the boys celebrate their single 'Flying Without Wings' reaching number one?

7) What was the name of the performing arts school Bryan went to?

8) Which Spice Girl does Shane like the most?

9) Who wished the boys the best of luck with their career at their first appearance on *Top Of The Pops*?

10) Where did the boys hold the launch party for Westside?

11) Who's Nicky favourite actress?

12) What's Shane's favourite food?

13) Which football team does Bryan support?

14) What was the name of the independent single IOU put out?

15) Who did Westlife knock off the number one spot in the charts with their second single, 'If I Let You Go'?

16) What does Shane's brother, Liam, do?

17) Who did Shane play in the Hawkswell Theatre production of *Grease* in 1996?

18) Who pestered Louis Walsh to become IOU's manager?

19) At what venue did IOU support the Backstreet Boys?

20) What three songs did they perform during their support slot on the Backstreet Boys tour?

21) Where were the auditions for the replacement member of IOU held?

22) How did Nicky record his demo tape for the audition?

23) Who's often referred to as the sixth member of Westlife?

24) Who is Westlife's stylist?

25) What well-respected songwriting duo wrote 'Swear It Again' and 'Flying Without Wings'?

26) Where did the boys record their debut album, *Westlife*?

27) What award did the boys win at the *Smash Hits* Poll Winners' Party in 1998?

28) Who presented them with their first *Smash Hits* golden disc?

29) What was the date of Westside's showcase for the UK media and members of the music industry?

30) How did Westlife amuse themselves in between recording in Sweden?

31) Name three groups who have also recorded at the Swedish studios.

32) In which country is Nicky most popular?

33) What's the fifth song on Westlife's debut album?

34) What was the name of the band Bryan was in before he auditioned for IOU?

35) Who is Mark's favourite female singer?

36) How many brothers and sisters does Bryan have?

37) Who do Westlife want to have a cameo appearance in their upcoming film?

38) What did Nicky want to be after he left Leeds United?

39) Who told Nicky about the auditions for IOU?

40) What have the boys agreed not to do for at least five years?

41) What would put Mark off a girl?

42) Name the original line-up of IOU.

43) What show did IOU appear in together?

44) Where did IOU arrange to meet Louis Walsh?

45) Who was the first A&R man to see IOU?

46) How many brothers and sisters does Nicky have?

47) What word do Westlife always say before going on stage?

48) Where were Westlife when they heard they'd won the *Smash Hits* Best New Tour Act award?

49) Who did they give their award to?

50) Which member of Westlife once snogged two cousins in one night?

51) Who stole from his best friend?

52) Who used to play with girls' toys?

53) Who used to snog his girlfriend's mates?

54) Who used to be dressed up like a girl?

55) Who once snogged eleven girls in one night?

56) Who once pretended to be a member of boy band OTT?

57) Who is Bryan's favourite actor?

58) What's the boys' favourite film ever?

59) What's Nicky's favourite cereal?

60) What would be Shane's dream home?

61) What perfume does Bryan like girls to wear?

62) Who is Shane's favourite actor?

63) Where is Nicky's favourite place to chill out?

64) What tattoo does Kian have?

65) Who's favourite song is Britney Spears' 'Baby, One More Time'?

66) How tall is Mark?

67) Who used to look at the ladies' lingerie in his mum's catalogues?

68) Who is Mark's favourite male singer?

69) Who flushed his mum's wedding rings down the toilet?

70) Why did Mark get told off by his girlfriend's parents?

71) Who once wore dirty knickers for three days on the trot?

72) What did Bryan used to collect?

73) What is Nicky most terrified about?

74) Who fell off a balcony and was saved by a washing line?

75) What is Kian's date of birth?

76) What is Shane's date of birth?

77) What is Nicky's date of birth?

78) What is Mark's date of birth?

79) What is Bryan's date of birth?

80) What music did Kian used to listen to when he was at school?

81) What got Kian interested in boy bands?

82) What did Mark and his family do every Sunday evening?

83) What went wrong the first time Shane and his friend had a rehearsal for a boy band?

84) What did Mark first want to be?

85) What was the name of the clothes shop where Nicky worked?

86) What phrase does Shane say most often?

87) Why couldn't Louis Walsh manage IOU to begin with?

88) What legendary pop producer worked on Westlife's album?

89) What have Westlife done that no other boy band has ever achieved?

90) Where were Westlife on 4 July 1999?

91) Where did Westlife film their video for 'If I Let You Go'?

92) Who do the boys ring if they're not sure what day it is?

93) How long did Nicky like Georgina before he did anything about it?

94) What made Mark laugh at the Irish launch party of 'Swear It Again'?

95) How many members of Westlife are not in serious relationships?

96) Who travelled on the Westlife tour bus with them when they supported Boyzone on tour?

97) Who gets the most fan mail?

98) What would put Kian off a girl?

99) Who does Bryan fancy out of *Friends*?

100) Who does Mark like the best out of Steps?

## How did you score?

1) Kian.

2) Because of his weight.

3) Because he was considered too small to be a goalie.

4) Louis spotted it on the side of a skip.

5) The Irish Prime Minister, Bertie Aherne.

6) They went out for a meal with some close friends.

7) Billy Barry's.

8) Posh Spice, Victoria Adams.

9) Martine McCutcheon.

10) At the Cafe De Paris in London.

11) Demi Moore.

12) Spaghetti.

13) Manchester United.

14) 'Together Girl Forever'.

15) Ronan Keating.

16) He runs a horse business with Shane's dad.

17) Danny.

18) Shane's mum, Mae.

19) The RDS Arena in Dublin.
20) 'Together Girl Forever', 'Everlasting Love' and 'Pinball Wizard'.
21) The Red Box in Dublin.
22) On his karaoke machine in his living room.
23) Anto Byrne, the band's tour manager.
24) Kenny Ho.
25) Stevie Mac and Wayne Hector.
26) At the Cheiron Studios in Stockholm, Sweden.
27) Best New Tour Act.
28) Stephen Gately from Boyzone.
29) Wednesday 3 February 1999.
30) They had snowball fights.
31) The Backstreet Boys, 'N Sync and Five.
32) Spain.
33) 'No No'.
34) Cartel.
35) Mariah Carey.
36) He has one sister.
37) Ronan Keating.
38) A policeman.
39) His auntie.
40) They've agreed not to get married or have babies for five years.
41) If she was picking her nose or had smelly breath.
42) Shane, Mark, Kian, Michael, Derek and Graham.
43) *Grease*.
44) The POD nightclub in Dublin.
45) Simon Cowell from RCA.
46) One brother and one sister.
47) 'Westlife'.

48) At Dublin airport.
49) Louis Walsh.
50) Mark.
51) Nicky.
52) Shane.
53) Shane.
54) Nicky.
55) Nicky.
56) Nicky.
57) Leo DiCaprio.
58) *Titanic*.
59) Sugar Puffs.
60) A very big place with a swimming pool.
61) Cool Water.
62) Tom Cruise.
63) On his couch in his living room.
64) The Chinese symbol for spirit and soul.
65) Kian's.
66) 5' 11".
67) Shane.
68) Michael Jackson.
69) Bryan.
70) For being a keen go-karter.
71) Shane.
72) He used to collect *Discovery* magazine.
73) Getting stuck in a lift.
74) Kian.
75) 29 April 1980.
76) 5 July 1979.
77) 9 October 1978.
78) 28 May 1980.

79) 12 April 1980.

80) He listened to Metallica, Guns N' Roses and Bon Jovi.

81) Hearing the kind of pop music Take That produced.

82) They used to go round to his grandparents' house and perform party pieces.

83) The other two members of the band didn't bother to turn up.

84) A professional tennis player.

85) Alias Tom.

86) 'You know what I mean.'

87) He was too busy managing Boyzone.

88) Max Martin.

89) Their first three singles have gone straight to number one in the UK charts.

90) In Hyde Park, performing at Party In The Park for the Prince's Trust.

91) In Tenerife in the Canary Islands.

92) They ring their mums.

93) Two years.

94) The sight of the Irish Prime Minister bopping away to Westlife's music.

95) Four of them.

96) Ronan Keating and Keith Duffy of Boyzone.

97) None of them do, the amount of fan mail they receive is pretty equal.

98) If she told him she fancied him because he was in Westlife.

99) Rachel.

100) Lisa.

## Conclusions: So, how did you do?

### If you scored 1–25:

**No No!** Oh dear, are you sure you didn't mean to pick up a book on the Corrs instead? Or did you just buy this book for the gorgeous pictures of the lads? Put Westlife on to your CD player, whack up the volume, turn to page 7 in this book and start reading it all over again – and make sure you pay attention this time. Oh, and repeat 'Westlife are brilliant' ten times before you go to bed.

### 26–50

**Try Again!** Not a bad score, but you could do better. You like the songs, and you know all five boys' names, but it's the little details that make up the whole picture, you know. You can't call yourself a true fan unless you know everything about the boys, from the time Nicky cried himself to sleep to what colour underpants Shane wears. Try repeating 'I will learn everything there is to know about Westlife' five times before you go to school in the mornings.

### 50–75

**Flying Without Wings!** You are a true Westlife fan. You know all their songs by heart, where they live and even the name of their childhood pets. Give yourself a pat on the back and rest assured in the knowledge that Nicky would probably be proud to introduce you to Georgina.

## 76–100

**We Are One!** Tell the truth now, either you are secretly related to one of the Westlife boys, you cheated, or you are quite simply the biggest Westlife fan in the world and probably know exactly what they're doing right this minute. Maybe you could get a job as their personal organizer...